DECORATIVE
DETAILS

DECORATIVE DETAILS

Essential ingredients for creating
the country look

JULES MACMAHON

COLLINS & BROWN

For David, Henry, Lucy and Flora,
with all my love.

First published in Great Britain in 2001
by Collins & Brown Limited
64 Brewery Road
London N7 9NT

A member of **Chrysalis** Books plc

Distributed in the United States and Canada by Sterling Publishing Co.,
387 Park Avenue South
New York
NY 10016 USA

Published in association with The National Magazine Company Limited.

1 3 5 7 9 8 6 4 2

British Library Cataloguing-in-Publication Data:
A catalogue record for this book is available from the British Library.

ISBN 1 84340 064 2

Conceived, edited and designed by Collins & Brown Limited

Editor: Gillian Haslam
Copy Editor: Alison Wormleighton
Designer: Christine Wood

Reproduction by Classic Scan Pte Ltd, Singapore
Printed and bound by Kyodo Printing Co Pte Ltd, Singapore

This book was typeset using Bauer Bodoni and Futura

Front cover photographs, from left to right:
Top row: Caroline Arber, Tom Leighton, Pia Tryde, Polly Wreford.
Bottom row: Polly Wreford, Caroline Arber, Caroline Arber.
Back cover photographs, from left to right:
Pia Tryde, James Merrell, Pia Tryde, Tham Nhu Tran.
Spine photograph: Caroline Arber.

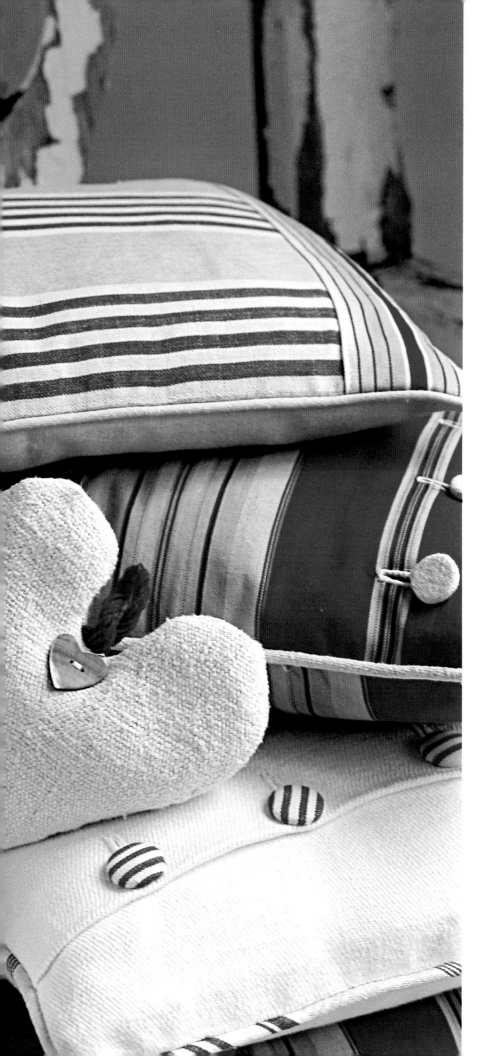

contents

introduction

Decorative schemes – be they in a room or in a garden – are compositions made up of myriad details, each one saying a great deal about the originator. No single element can be dismissed as irrelevant, for each adds to or detracts from the whole. So, for the decorator or gardener aiming to create what may loosely be described as a country look, the canvas is indeed vast. Yet by following certain tenets as you add details layer by layer, you cannot fail. Use natural materials – they look beautiful and they weather well. Do not compromise on quality. Let form follow function, avoiding unnecessary fussiness. Choose hand-made over mass-produced, and allow the hands and

minds of the craftspeople to show through in all their diversity. With these

guidelines informing your scheme, you will be off to a fine start, but take care

not to become a prisoner of rigid rules. The intrinsic rightness of any room

owes much to the imagination of its owner, so feel free to experiment.

As you will see from the pages that follow, the sparest of drawing rooms can

be transformed by a single beautiful looking-glass or an inventively displayed

collection. An unexceptional bedroom can become a glorious retreat of crisp

linens and soft quilting, and the most clinical of kitchens given a much needed

warmth by adding a row of gleaming copper pans. With authenticity, simplicity

and beauty as your bywords, your decorative schemes are bound to succeed.

Hard Surfaces

The walls and floors of a room present a challenge: they are the largest expanses of colour and pattern and must actually work as durable surfaces too. Get these right and you have an accommodating framework into which to introduce furniture, fabrics and decorative details. Do take your time with these important backdrops. Never underestimate the power of a change of tone on a painted wall – for every shade of sunny yellow there is a ghastly egg-yolk hue waiting to ambush you.

The successful marriage of hard surfaces – floor, walls, ceiling and furniture – in this splendidly solid hallway seems almost effortless. In fact, each element works both independently and as part of the whole. The flagstones worn to an idiosyncratic camber by two centuries of human traffic are both handsome and eminently practical. The calm neutrals of the paintwork on walls and ceiling lift the eye from the dark floor and are the perfect foil for the pine of the haberdasher's chest and the soft earth tones of the wooden bowl and cider flagon. The flat unfussiness of the painted walls also manages to diminish the impact of the pipes. Three details – the bulrushes, seedheads and simply framed crewelwork – balance the hallway by adding softness without compromising its autumnal colour scheme of conker and dead leaf.

Painted walls

By far the quickest way to create an impact or change the atmosphere in a room is to paint the walls in a solid colour (and if your choice is a disaster, it's easily remedied with a few more pots of paint). This flexibility means you can take a risk: there's no need to be straightjacketed by accepted wisdom. Your choice of colour may be an inspired one, or the room's size, shape and lighting may result in serendipitous success. As a general rule, a 'lived in' look is more easily achieved with flatter colours which have a limey or chalky finish, rather than shiny vinyls which have often sacrificed that satisfying depth of colour present in traditionally produced paints. Whatever your preferences, the rapidly expanding range of finishes and colours now available means you needn't compromise.

AN ETHEREAL DELFT BLUE is most appropriate for an attic bedroom in the clouds. Sensibly, in a room with slightly awkward angles at the roofline, the blue continues onto the ceiling, avoiding any ugly 'joins'. The freshness and simplicity of the colour scheme marry perfectly with the pine furniture and the folksy quilt and gingham cushion.

LILAC IS A MUCH UNDERRATED SHADE, valuable for both its warmth and its freshness. Here it is used on a door architrave to provide an echo of the shade in the hallway beyond. The solid blocks of colour on the hallway walls – lilac above, cream below – are interesting but plain enough to avoid a fight with the highly polished tiled floor.

Dados and skirtings

Quite often, architectural necessities provide balance and detail in a room. The dado rail, designed to run around an interior wall at just about the height of a chair back to give protection from scuffs, also serves to split the wall up into potentially interesting spaces. The area above the dado rail does not get a great deal of wear and tear, but below the rail the dado is subject to knocks from passing feet, prams and bicycles (which is one reason it was traditionally darker). The dado is sometimes papered with a tough Anaglypta wallpaper prior to painting. The skirting bridges the junction between floor and wall as well as protecting a vulnerable area. It looks excellent as a plain board in simple interiors or as a more elaborately moulded rail in grander rooms.

The clever decorator can exploit these functional details to create any number of striking wall effects.

TAKE COURAGE FROM THE ADVENTUROUS USE OF COLOUR that works so successfully on these bedroom walls. A strong sunny yellow warms the room above the dado rail and is strikingly partnered by a vibrant shade of lilac beneath. The unusual combination is smartly edged by a crisp white dado rail and skirting.

RESTRAINED NEUTRALS WORK WONDERFULLY on Georgian interiors and contemporary minimalist schemes alike. Here, cream and taupe are divided by a neat trompe l'oeil dado rail in pale yellow that sings out as if illuminated.

Take a couple of shades from a group of similar tones to make a harmonious and understated blend, perhaps just separated by a plain white dado rail; or go right to the other extreme and combine a bold and vibrant dark-hued dado with an equally flamboyant light shade above.

If your free time (or budget) is limited, simply pick a gloriously bright colour that complements your existing wall colours, and use it to smarten up the dado rail, skirting and perhaps door frame. This will completely alter the look of your room and even how you perceive the wall colours.

No dado rail? Lengths of moulded rail are inexpensive and easy to attach to the wall, and they come in a variety of designs. Or simply go faux: with measuring tape and spirit level in hand, you can apply a narrow band of paint that looks extremely effective.

A FORMAL HALLWAY IS GIVEN A DASH OF MODERN IRREVERENCE with the unusual combination of lilac above the dado rail and cream below separated by a warm terracotta red. The red used again in the skirting blends well with the floor.

A SMALL, DARK BREAKFAST ROOM IS LIFTED DRAMATICALLY with bicoloured yellow walls. Used alone, the upper shade would have been overpowering, the lower insipid, but combined they work well. The dado rail has gone, and the skirting exists only as a plain narrow board, as befits the simplicity of this room.

Painted stripes

Striped walls can take on many guises: narrow, boldly coloured stripes create a formal finish; smudgy, homespun ones are comfortable and relaxed. The obvious way to achieve stripes that are exactly the right colour and width for your own walls is to paint them yourself. Certainly you will find a plethora of striped wallpapers, and these may suit your purpose best if you are going for a very crisp, 'finished' look. But if you crave a more individual style (and are quite happy to avoid the extra expense and necessary expertise of hanging paper) then paint-it-yourself is an excellent option. Provided you arm yourself with a good tape measure and plenty of masking tape, painting stripes is not difficult. If you prefer your stripes to fade into one another, don't use masking tape, just follow a faint marked line and brush the two colours gently into one another as they meet.

Do remember that the type of stripes you choose will affect the way you perceive the proportions of your room. Narrow, bold vertical stripes tend to raise the ceiling visually, making the room look taller and thinner, while wide horizontal stripes of colour give the illusion of squatter walls and a lower ceiling.

Bands of colour running horizontally around a room are innovative in a contemporary decorative scheme and great fun in a child's playroom – add a few notes and a treble clef for the musical child, or attach simple coloured wooden shelves that match up with each stripe for storing books and toys.

THE FREE AND UNFUSSY STYLE OF THESE PAINTED STRIPES accords well with the rough plaster wall surface – it would be both impossible and inappropriate to aim for set-square accuracy here. Instead, the slightly translucent wash in warm terracotta and ochre yellow shows off the natural idiosyncrasies of the wall. The fat vertical stripes also seem to lower the ceiling, making the atmosphere of this sitting room snug and intimate.

Stencilling and stamping

These two essential techniques are everything that decorative details should be: simple to add to a room, instantly effective and infinitely variable. Whether used separately or together, the techniques of stencilling and stamping are invaluable allies in the process of transforming any decorative scheme.

Stencil kits are widely available in a veritable library of designs, from crisp geometric patterns to a profusion of flowers, ribbons and boughs; alternatively, draw and cut out your own stencils. Stamp motifs are similarly easy to obtain.

Stamping is excellent if you want a subtle overall pattern in a painted room, and is tremendous when you have to deal with irksome nooks and crannies which would not welcome wallpaper. Stencilling can accentuate architectural details, such as a doorway, skirting board or cornice, or highlight the placing of special furniture – a carved bedhead perhaps.

STENCILLED RIBBONS AND FLOWERS cascade around a door frame. The delicacy of the painting sits beautifully against the softly mottled walls in the same colour tones and adds movement and interest to the whole area around the door.

THIS CLASSIC STAR STAMP is decorative without being too frilly and feminine. In fact, it is hard to think of a room in which it would be inappropriate, be it child's bedroom or a formal study. The white stars on the chalky lilac ground are a perfect foil for the display of plates in complementary shades.

NEUTRALS CREATE A CALM ATMOSPHERE that can be added to without disruption by introducing a delicate stencil (in this case, an olive branch along the top of the panelling) in the same colour family.

Wallpapers

Wallpaper has been in use in country homes for several hundred years, initially in the form of hand-blocked sheets (though it only became fashionable in the early 1700s, when flocked papers imitating expensive textiles were introduced). Rolls of wallpaper as we know them didn't appear until more than a century later.

Today's wallpaper patterns can be based on anything from ancient Japanese textiles to 1960s' psychedelia: they may mimic nature or paint effects. The range is often bewildering but those traditional staples of country style – florals, stripes, checks, the odd bucolic scene – are enduringly popular.

Beware, however: instant pattern is a double-edged sword. A little sample of cheery sprigged paper may appear charming, but an entire wall, or room, of it could quickly send you running for the door. Try to get a large sample of the wallpaper. It may even be more economical in the long run to order a whole roll and see how the paper looks in different areas of the room – in strong light by a window, or butting up to a dark fireplace, for example.

The advantage of wallpaper is that it gives a finished, furnished look to any room, and can bring in glorious patterns and depths of colour that can be difficult to achieve in any other format.

HE WHO DARES SOMETIMES WINS: this rich ruby washday-motif wallpaper could easily become overpowering in a small area, but succeeds in a spacious dining room used sparingly above the plain white panelling.

WASTE NOT, WANT NOT. Small offcuts of sprigs, stripes and stars wallpaper in similar tones make excellent linings for drawers and shelves.

Tiled walls

Vivid colours, deep reflective glazes, satisfyingly nubbly textures: tiles are not only excellent from a purely decorative perspective, but are also highly functional on the walls of any room that is subject to extremes of temperature, water splashes and so on. As a detail, a few tiles can be made to work very hard by creating a dramatic pattern around a sink, mirror or kitchen range, or as canvasses for perfect little pictures themselves. Some of the most desirable of today's tiles are almost like small sculptures in clay with relief effects within the hand-painted decoration. Plain tiles look wonderful in multicoloured chequerboards *à la* 1950s' retro, while traditionalists will find that the soft blues and whites of English delftware or the deeply hued glazed tiles of Provence suit a period house well.

ARRANGED AROUND AN OVEN, handmade tiles in all their rich diversity of texture and colour glow umber, green, ochre and terracotta. Not just a pretty face, tiling also provides a durable, heat-resistant work surface and surround.

THE RICH MID-GREEN AND ANCIENT WHITE of these typically Provençal tiles work well in a simple chequerboard design around a sink. The majolica style of glazing gives a hard-wearing gloss surface.

Wooden flooring

If yours is an older house, you probably already have wooden floors. If they are lurking beneath old carpet or linoleum, rip it up! As perhaps the most practical and beautiful of all floors, wood deserves to be seen. Whether sealed, waxed, colourwashed or painted, it has warmth, durability and character. Wood is far healthier to live with than carpet and there is a huge range of shades and grains from nature's unbeatable pattern book.

The boards of structural floors are most often softwood such as pine, but overlay floors (such as strip flooring, wood blocks or parquet) are hardwood. A hardwood like oak makes eminently practical close-grained floorboards; walnut has a darker heartwood that works splendidly in a formal dining room; maple has creamy, honeyed tones with the odd bird's-eye whirl; cherry's reddish-brown tinge is warm and welcoming; while blond ash and birch are light and modern.

If laying a new floor, you can choose not just the species but also the grade, from plain straight grains to rustic grades with colour variation, knots and burrs. Make sure the wood comes from a sustainable source – or consider using salvaged wood flooring.

SIMPLE WIDE FLOORBOARDS have been sanded and then treated with a woodwax to which colour pigments have been added. This is easy to clean and it wears well: in a hallway like this which takes a great deal of traffic, the worn areas can just be rewaxed occasionally.

A DIAMOND FLOOR PATTERN in Scandinavian grey-blue and white looks decorative and also helps this landing appear wider. Plain boards laid across a narrow room have the same effect.

Tiled floors

When decorating or refurbishing a country home, you cannot fail if you turn to nature for materials and inspiration – and perhaps nowhere is this more true than with tiled floors, whether quarried or fired in a kiln.

Natural stone like slate, marble and limestone is simply quarried and then worked into shape. Traditionally, slate is split by hand for a superb surface finish, and comes in the familiar silvery blue as well as greens and ochres. It is supremely durable in areas of heavy traffic like halls and kitchens.

The mellow pinks, burgundies and buffs of terracotta (unglazed earthenware) just get better as the years go by, and the special variegated effects seem to intensify with age. This too is exceptionally hard-wearing. (If time is short, consider ceramic tiles, which can mimic terracotta fairly convincingly and require far less maintenance.) Just about all tiled floors can be found in salvaged form today, so your 'new' terracotta floor could predate your house by a century or two, and have its origins in a Tuscan barn or Mexican hacienda.

Encaustic tiles are ceramic tiles with a pattern made from a different-coloured clay inlaid into the surface; when fired, the two meld together. They are often seen in Victorian geometric-patterned pathways, but encaustic tiles come in all shapes and shades and are just as good inside the house.

OLD TERRACOTTA TILES used in a completely plain way in a country kitchen. Reclaimed flooring suits a period house well, and does not need any 'wearing in' to look at home. As with all tiled floors, spills mop up easily, dog hairs and food do not cling and the room is generally quick and simple to keep clean.

A NATURAL STONE FLOOR has great tonal variety and harmony, and its calm greys balance out the fairly busy pattern on the walls of this sitting room. Anyone who sees its chips, dips and bumps as defects rather than characterful attributes should go for carpet!

Natural floor coverings

A rug, runner or mat is an effective decorative detail: thrown down in a moment, it can contribute greatly to the comfort and colour scheme of a room. Particularly popular today are the natural-fibre floor coverings – seagrass, coir, jute, sisal and paper – whose simplicity and stylishness allow them to fit into any room scheme, contemporary or farmhouse traditional.

Chinese seagrass, grown in paddy fields and then dried and spun into yarn, deserves a special mention for being stain-resistant. However, this non-absorbency means that it can't be dyed, so you are limited to its natural beige and brown.

Coir is familiar as everyone's doormat, but this fibre removed from the coconut husk is soaked in salty water to soften it and then pounded and combed out before being woven. Its natural colouring depends on the time of year it was harvested. Although coir is praised for its tactile qualities, many people find it positively prickly, so it's not the best floor covering for bedrooms or young children's playrooms. It is, however, ideal for areas of heavy traffic.

Jute has its origins in rope-making and is the fibrous inner bark of a large plant that is soaked, sun-dried and then spun. The resulting yarn is particularly silky, so it can be used where bare feet will pad around. However, it is not particularly hard-wearing.

Sisal, which comes from the crushed leaves of an agave plant, is the most lustrous of the natural fibres, and it is also hard-wearing. It can be dyed any colour, but the downside of this is that it stains easily. In fact, sisal, along with coir and jute, should be treated with stain-repellent after being laid, especially if you have chosen a pale colour.

Paper, spun from softwood pulp, with resin added at this stage, and then twisted into threads which are waxed and woven, produces a durable, moisture-resistant floor covering of surprising versatility. It can also be combined with sisal.

Do not forget wool: not in its much-maligned (and rightly so) shag-pile form, but in exciting, superbly textured flatweaves that make the most of its softness, warmth and resiliency. What is more, wool combines beautifully with some of the plant fibres – woven with a sisal weft, or mixed with jute, for example – to create a subtle and stylish statement.

A FLATWEAVE WOOL RUNNER in subtle greys and welcoming reds is perfect by the front door. This method of spinning and weaving the wool produces a texture reminiscent of the plant-fibre coverings, and gives it a pleasingly rural character.

Ceilings

If something that is above your head can be overlooked, then that is often what happens with a ceiling. Generally, decorators just slap on some white paint because that's what everyone usually does and luckily a light colour is often exactly what a room needs. Unless a ceiling is particularly special in some way – perhaps it has wonderful exposed beams, cornicing or panelling, or an intricate centre rose – then it often goes unnoticed, only being remarked upon if some decorative faux pas has been committed.

Unfortunately, certain ceiling trends from recent years now cause many a groan. The swirly royal-icing effect of textured plaster has lost its charm and is not easy to remove. Polystyrene ceiling tiles installed decades ago are now unwelcome house guests. False ceilings that were sometimes put in place to hide cracks or damaged cornicing or to allow for recessed lighting are simply oppressive and spoil the original proportions of a room. If wrong, ceilings are expensive to put right, but hugely worth it. As one of the most important 'bones' of the room's skeleton, a ceiling in harmony with the room beneath it pulls everything together.

IF YOUR ORIGINAL CEILING IS INTACT, then gently accentuate its special points. Here the ceiling is washed a soft blue and the old beams simply painted white. Light, airy colours make the ceiling seem higher and maximize any sunlight. If your room is too narrow and tall, a warm colour overhead creates the optical illusion of a lower ceiling and a more intimate atmosphere.

A TOUCH OF WHITE between these splendid rafters and beams is all that was needed. The simple rusticity of this sitting room is accentuated by exposing the architectural framework of the house, and leaving the warm tones of the wood to speak for themselves.

Painted furniture

This form of decorative detailing has to be one of the most creative and satisfying of all. Imagine your wooden furniture as a blank canvas: you can transform any piece, be it a tiny box or a giant bedstead, and it may entail anything from adding just a touch of pattern to changing the entire surface.

The range of possible finishes and techniques that can be used is staggering. It includes simple freehand painting if you have even a glimmer of artistic talent, stencilling, gilding, crackling, graining, distressing, and faux finishes like metal, marble, tortoiseshell, stucco, leather, verdigris, woodgrain – name it and there's a way of faking it. Many of these sound as if you need a professional qualification to achieve success, but there are a number of excellent books available with step-by-step instructions, so don't feel intimidated.

Painting your furniture is not just a way of giving vent to creative talent, it is also a highly cost-effective way of bringing basically sound but unlovely pieces back to life, and adapting them to the style and colour scheme of your room. Luckily for the furniture painter, many thousands of these appealingly unfussy tables, chairs, boxes and cupboards were made in relatively cheap pine to furnish servants' quarters and small Victorian houses, and these excellent candidates for decorative treatment are now easy to track down. Your attic, car-boot sales and market stalls can all be sources of furniture and decorative accessories that would be overlooked by

COMPLETELY UNPRETENTIOUS AND WELL-WEATHERED, this sturdy cupboard in distressed shades of pale blue and green is perfect for a farm cottage and is capacious enough for its purpose.

A MASTERPIECE OF INVENTION AND PAINTERLY TALENT: this kitchen cupboard was built from reclaimed doors and edged with stair spindles. The faded duck-egg blue is a perfect background for the panels decorated with birds and flowers which were inspired by traditional Indian paintings.

THIS JUNK-SHOP SIDE TABLE HAS BEEN PAINTED IN WHITE AND PALE YELLOW emulsion and sanded back gently to let the grain of the wood show through. Pine furniture was traditionally the cheap and cheerful alternative to 'good' woods, and as a result many a simple, rustic pine piece was discarded when a better one could take its place.

anyone who does not have a paintbrush and imagination at the ready. Don't be put off by ghastly shades of gloss paint or unattractive wood; you can rejuvenate the most forlorn kitchen chair or simple little cupboard. Just make sure it is not too wobbly and that the shape appeals to you – the rest can be improved.

As with many decorating projects, preparation is all-important. The surfaces of your wood have to be cleaned well and sanded down if you are not simply painting a design onto an acceptable background. Sanding is not the most pleasant of tasks as it can take a long time and create a lot of dust – speed it up by hiring an electric sander if you have a large area to cover.

Then on to the fun part: applying your paint. Depending on the finish you want, you may have to apply several layers, perhaps using a crackle varnish to give the 'aged' look that sits so happily in many period homes, or sanding back particular areas that would naturally receive more wear and tear over the years (corners, around handles and so on) to reveal slightly different shades of paint beneath.

Adding decorative motifs can be done freehand: just keep the design simple if you are unsure of your painting skills. Stencilling creates an attractive folk art look, while stamping is extremely quick and effective (refer to pages 22-23 for further details on both of these techniques). This is the beauty of customizing furniture – the complexity of the project is completely up to you.

A FRAME FOR A PLATE RACK has been cunningly fashioned from a carved skirting board which has received a wash of pale blue to complement the splash-back tiles. The painting on the edges of the kitchen shelves lifts the mundane into the highly ornamental: simple zigzags, dots and diamonds look both rustic and exotically ethnic.

A STYLIZED LEAF DESIGN – the simplest of stencils – floats on a folding table painted in flat green and yellow emulsions and unevenly sanded to allow varying amounts of colour to show through.

Wooden tables and chairs

It is not only floors for which wood is a natural winner: a room furnished with mellow wooden pieces like tables, dressers and chairs is always inviting and homely. The addition of even just one of these items as a decorative detail can add charm and atmosphere to any corner of a room.

Although a formal dining room looks splendid with a large Georgian dining table and a matching set of chairs and carvers, you would have to break the bank for a set of mahogany Chippendale ribbonback chairs, or indeed anything remotely associated with them. A more relaxed look for a kitchen or breakfast room can be achieved with simple bar-backed or comb-backed beech chairs or slightly more ornate ladderback armchairs with comfortable rush seats. Like the Windsor chair, bentwood furniture – in which rods of wood are bent into pleasing curves after being heated with steam – is always popular.

Sturdy pine furniture is a natural choice for country homes. It is still readily available as vast amounts of it were made from the 1850s onwards to fit out kitchens and servants' quarters. Because the pine came from Britain, Scandinavia and North America, antique pieces appear in a huge variety of shades and grains.

Oak refectory tables with planked tops and stretchers look superb in farmhouse kitchens with benches and settles for seats, while old serving tables make excellent smaller breakfast tables.

GENTLY ROUNDED ELM AND ASH CHAIRS add their natural tones to a room where wood dominates, and contrast with the straight edges of door, ceiling beams, floor and table. Most pine tables are today left stripped and waxed to show off the natural shades and grains of the wood, but at the time when they were made, in the latter part of the 18th century, they were generally painted.

A DINING ROOM INFUSED WITH THE ESSENCE OF 'SHABBY CHIC'. The charming little rustic table is surrounded by a set of hall chairs stained in green and painted to highlight the whimsical cut-outs.

Comfort Zones

To each of us, our home is a special place. It is our *sanctum sanctorum*, our safe retreat from the knocks and buffets of the outside world. As such, we all want our homes to be places of comfort and beauty where we can totally relax, and refresh the mind and spirit too. Fortunately, there is a plethora of decorative details that can be added to bedrooms, bathrooms and sitting rooms – the zones we put aside for rest and comfort – which will increase the pleasure of simply being at home.

Fabric is all-important, for both colour and texture; indeed, it is often the decorative focal point of a room. Simple details like adding or changing curtain tie-backs or cushions or re-covering an armchair can alter and improve the nature of any of these comfort zones, but particularly the sitting room. The bedroom should be a place of tranquillity, crisp white linens, soft quilts and welcoming pillows. In the bathroom, just changing the accessories and adding piles of towels can make bathing a much more enjoyable experience and the bathroom more of a place to linger.

Winter-weight curtains

Closing the curtains on a gusty winter's night is like letting down the portcullis in your own personal castle. The door is bolted, the curtains drawn, and the cold and dark kept firmly at bay. Heavy curtains provide privacy, they keep the heat in and the draughts out, and they add their own atmosphere of delightfully padded comfort to the decorative scheme. Interlining makes curtains hang beautifully and gives pleats and edges an attractive soft fullness.

You may prefer the cheerfulness of chintz or linen, the luxury of velvet or the sturdy warmth of wool – perhaps even in rug or blanket form rather than conventional curtains. But whatever your choice, decide in advance whether the curtains are to be the 'busy' area of your room. They may take up an entire wall, especially if they fall to the floor, and thus become the dominant feature. If the curtains are heavily patterned, keep the walls plain or softly patterned, and vice versa.

If your curtains currently hang on a functional track, consider changing to a carved wooden pole for a rural touch, and adding tapes or rings. If there is no pelmet, a simple length of fabric or even an old silk scarf or shawl twisted around a pole can look wonderful.

A WOOL RUG IN A TRADITIONAL NAVAJO DESIGN looks completely at home used as a portière, draped across this wooden door to block out winter draughts. The strong reds and oranges suit the pale tones of door and clock, and highlight the polished doorknob. The 'wild west' beauty of the rug is continued in the beaten iron of the pole and finial, and in the no-fuss attachment by the rug's own fringes. A masculine leather belt used as a tie-back completes the picture.

COMPLETELY FEMININE, these sumptuous chintz curtains with their bold yellows and purples sit well against the soft lilac wall. They are deliberately overlong to fall in elegant puddles of fabric that not only look charming but also act as efficient insulators.

Translucent curtains

Translucent curtains filter the light without blocking it, producing a soft atmosphere well suited to a period home. Forget all connotations of twitching nets and instead consider the beauties of lace. Whether bobbin, needle or filet lace, and whether made from cotton, silk, linen or wool, the intricate delicacy of this fabric makes it superb as a sheer curtain. Perhaps you have an antique lace shawl or tablecloth that would look excellent clipped over a window using café clips, or just suspended over the lower half of a large sash window, framed by fixed draperies. In the late 19th century, long panels of lace were made to hang flat at a floor-to-ceiling or French window, giving a degree of privacy without hiding the architecture of the window frame or the view beyond, and this treatment looks just as good today.

If not lace, try muslin, a plain-woven cotton fabric which is extremely fine and smooth in texture; it is also very economical, so you can drape it lavishly around your windows without having to think about the cost. Muslin is sometimes patterned in the loom, machine-embroidered or printed with dots or fragile sprigging. Batiste, a sheer fine muslin that has been mercerized, is also worth trying. Gauzes and voiles are other contenders for translucent window dressing. As an alternative to conventional sheers, you could simply loop different-coloured lengths of muslin or voile in contrasting or toning colours over poles; some lengths can be allowed to hang loose and others knotted at the centre for further interest.

To vary the amount of light let in, try layering sheer fabrics: perhaps one could be fixed across the entire pane of glass, and a second used as a loosely twisted pelmet or draped around the window as a frame. Layering also works well if you mix translucent fabrics with fixed heavy curtains.

A SHEER LACE PANEL LETS LIGHT FLOOD IN, diffused at the sides by ta creamy-toned bedspread edged with lace and held back by a tasselled rope tie-back.

THE ELEGANT PROPORTIONS AND ORIGINAL WOODEN SHUTTERS of this window are shown off to their best advantage by the simple addition of a panel of antique lace. The fragile whiteness of the lace tablecloth echoes the window treatment.

Decorative curtain details

If the curtains of your choice are already in place, but you feel they still lack a certain style or charm, there are plenty of ways to dress them up a little or freshen the look. Perhaps the most obvious is to add some kind of edging to the fabric: binding tape, ribbon, rope or a simple fringe or braid in a different colour is easily attached. Alternatively, you could add a deep border in a contrasting fabric to the lower edge, or an integral valance in a coordinating fabric to the top edge.

Another option is to line the curtain with a different fabric: a strong gingham could be backed with a faded floral, or stripes backed with a corresponding plain fabric. Not only is this understated addition as eye-catching as a flash of lime silk lining on a sober city suit, but it gives the curtains more body.

Also easy and fun are unexpected tie-backs, such as simple ribbons tied in a loose bow, silk flowers tucked

A SHOCKINGLY GOOD COMBINATION: fresh cobalt blue gingham curtains are trimmed with a startling fuchsia-pink cotton moss fringe. The pink is picked up in a fat posy of velvet pansies tucked into a plain velvet ribbon tie-back.

AN ANTIQUE MONOGRAMMED LINEN TOWEL lets in just the right amount of light and is combined with a modern peony-red gingham to make a practical and unusual blind.

into tie-backs, plain thick rope knotted around a heavy linen curtain, or curvy wrought iron in contemporary shapes.

Changing the way curtains are suspended can alter their character. Dull metal or plastic tracking can be exchanged for a pole wrought by a smith into virtually any shape you care to name, coupled with rings in colours ranging from solid black to verdigris. Or change the heading, substituting something like ties, tabs or jumbo eyelets, all of which are used with a pole or rod. Even if you can't sew, you'll soon find a curtain alteration service, or you could go for the easiest option of all and use metal curtain clips.

If a window has a blind that looks more boring than subtle, liven it up with a couple of dress curtains. These, as the name suggests, do not close – they just sit looking decorative (and therefore do not require huge amounts of fabric).

A BRIGHT CHECKED FABRIC has been given a stylish touch with a plain-coloured tab-and-button heading hung from an iron pole.

THE DELICACY OF A LACE TRIM along the centre of a sash window is emphasized by fragile antique crystal droplets attached to the points of the fabric – the work of a few minutes with dazzling results.

Natural light

Ever since the first primitive building was erected, getting sunlight indoors has been a consideration – a problem made easier to solve by the invention of glass. Sunlight uplifts us and fills us with energy, and we work better in conditions of natural light. Colours are their most true when seen in daylight – who does not take a pot of paint or a fabric swatch to a window to gauge the real colour? Light is symbolic of new beginnings, hope, divinity: think of Stonehenge at dawn, or the light falling on a church altar. None of this is surprising when we consider that the sun has been our primary light source for millennia, and it is only comparatively recently that we have been able to increase light levels in the home with a burst of gas, or flick of a switch.

Even today, when planning the general light levels you want in any room, you must be aware of natural light. Its unpredictability is part of its charm, even in climates with overcast skies for much of the winter and part of the summer. It does, nevertheless, generally follow certain patterns: north-facing rooms get a gentle, constant light with little glare, while south-facing rooms receive more direct sunlight in the wintertime when the sun is low in the sky (the opposite is true in the southern hemisphere). Rooms with a westerly outlook catch the heat of the afternoon sun and the reddish glow of sunset; east-facing rooms come to life in the early morning. When planning artificial lighting to fulfil the jobs of creating ambient, task and accent lighting, don't forget to allow for the ebb and flow of the sun's light around your house.

A PALE LIME GREEN DECORATES THIS CONSERVATORY which is used for meals on days when the air is just a little too fresh for comfort. Natural light floods in from all sides, benefiting both the diners and the seedlings potted on for the garden.

DAYLIGHT STREAMS INTO A PORCH, illuminating the splendid Victorian encaustic tiles. The stained glass changes the colours of natural daylight, adding its own subtle tones.

If you have a particularly dark and difficult area to light, and you crave natural daylight to dispel the gloom, consider installing a daylighting system. This utilizes indirect natural light by positioning mirrors – sometimes solar-powered, sun-tracking mirrors – so as to redirect sunlight into a reflective light-well and onto a diffusing lens. (The Victorians had their own version of this for windows facing onto dark, narrow alleys: a simple mirror was mounted on the outside wall to reflect light down into the dingy room.) A daylighting system minimizes the amount of artificial light needed, making it a highly energy-efficient light source.

Decoration and furnishings can also help to maximize the amount of light in a dark room: white surfaces reflect back about 90 per cent of the light they receive, grey paint about 50 per cent and fabrics only 35 per cent of light on average.

Do beware of the power of sunlight to fade and damage delicate surfaces: antique fabrics and fine old wooden furniture should not be exposed to strong direct sunlight. A gentle light diffused through translucent curtains or blinds is safer.

Conservatories and sunrooms have become extremely popular in the last few years: everyone wants to take advantage of as much natural daylight as possible. And sitting in your own personal glasshouse after sunset, you can still enjoy the natural light of the moon and stars.

AN EAST-FACING KITCHEN WORKS WONDERFULLY: the morning light streams in to get everyone off to a flying start, and cooking in the evening can be completed in a cooler atmosphere when the sun has moved away.

Sofas and armchairs

At the end of a good long walk (or a bad day at the office) there is no more welcoming sight when you reach home than that of a long drink placed next to a large, deep armchair or sofa which beckons you to sink into its forgiving contours. Fragile giltwood chairs or formal little Louis XV settees may look charming perched against a wall, but for pure relaxation we generally crave more robust seating: something that can be collapsed onto with impunity.

The classic upholstered sofa or armchair comes in myriad styles and shapes such as the deep and comfortable wing chair and bergère armchair; traditional chesterfields upholstered in leather with button-backs and rolled arms; the Knole settee with its characteristic drop ends, often handsomely tasselled; or the more unusual camel-back settee with its dromedary-like contours. The mahogany or walnut frame is sometimes

exposed and carved, often with padding on the arms, but generally the completely upholstered look is the most comfortable and homely.

Sofas sit well grouped around the fire, or facing one another across a low table or upholstered stool, and the benefits of a deep wing chair next to the fireplace mean warm feet without a hot head. The presence of country elements like a real fire, dogs and cats and muddy shoes means that, if country house sofas and armchairs are to look good and last well, they must be upholstered in sturdy fabrics – linens, gently faded chintzes, practical checks and tickings, and glowing damasks.

Large sofas and armchairs naturally take centre stage in a drawing or sitting room, but the bay of a window is perfect for an elegant *chaise longue* on which to recline gracefully, and a private little corner makes an excellent home for the curvaceous lines of a loveseat.

THIS ELEGANT AND COMFORTABLE WING CHAIR, rescued from an untimely demise in a junk shop, was stripped of its unappealing fabric and dressed in old linen sheets that show off its handsome lines well. The little cushion covered in antique linen with smart and simple buttons adds to the uncluttered look.

THE DEPTH OF THE SEAT IN THIS LOW ARMCHAIR makes this one of the most comfortable styles in which to relax. The red cotton ticking cover has a split personality: its tough simplicity makes it enviably hard-wearing, while the stripes add a touch of formal elegance.

LOW, OVERSTUFFED SOFAS AND ARMCHAIRS upholstered in muted floral patterns are the staples of the country drawing room. They are completely welcoming and perfectly decorative.

CHEERFUL CHECKS IN A COOL SCANDINAVIAN BLUE on this practical daybed are a good counterpoint to the warm terracotta and yellow walls and the large cushions and pillows covered in a soft peach fabric.

LOOKING AS UTTERLY AT HOME on a chair as its canine occupant, this traditional kilim brings rich patterns and vibrantly warm colours into a pale contemporary sitting room.

Warm colours and textures

As sofas and armchairs are generally large pieces of furniture, their colour scheme can dominate a room, and so this is a decorative detail that must be chosen with care. Perhaps the most welcoming of palettes for restful chairs and sofas is the range of warm colours.

An old-fashioned colour wheel can be a useful device for picking out warm hues and those that work well with them. The wheel consists of the colours of the spectrum arranged in a circle. The three primary colours are equally spaced around it, and between each pair of primaries is the secondary colour made by mixing them. Red and blue combine to make purple, blue and yellow make green, and yellow and red make orange. Other colours around the wheel, the tertiaries, are mixtures of these. Sometimes the tonal values made by adding white, grey or black to the basic hues are shown as additional rings around the central circle.

The colours on one half of the wheel – the yellows, oranges and reds – are the warm colours. Red is perhaps the most dominant. It makes objects seem larger (a red armchair will appear bigger than its blue twin) and, as with all warm hues, it appears to advance towards you, unlike the receding blues and greens on the other half of the wheel. All colours have a 'temperature': red is hot, pink is warm and comfortable, orange vibrant and lively, yellow mellow and sunny.

When choosing your fabric, bear in mind the textures that lend themselves to warm hues. Old kilims especially are full of the natural colours of spice and terracotta, and rich fabrics like velvet and damask look superb in plum, deep rose and burgundy.

Loose covers

Loose covers are to furniture what comfortable sweaters are to our wardrobes. Relaxed, hard-wearing and easy-going, they are not pulled tight to show every curve but hang casually in a forgiving way. And of course loose covers are, above all, immensely practical: you need never worry about spilt drinks when the covers can simply be removed for cleaning, particularly if the fabric has been treated with a stain-repellent finish. Do check, however, that your fabric is not prone to shrinking or it will be a struggle to replace them. Have two sets made at the same time if you can, in case of major damage to one set of covers that will take a while to repair. You may wish to have the second set made in a different colour or pattern – by changing the covers, you can give the room a completely different look in a matter of minutes.

Traditionally, loose covers are made in linen union or cotton, and you need around 8 metres (9 yards) of fabric for an average-sized armchair. Don't feel hidebound about choosing the fabric – as we have seen in the previous section, old linen sheets can work perfectly as long as the structure of the fabric is still sound and strong. You could even consider old linen tablecloths or a patchwork of traditional linen tea towels for an unusual and inexpensive loose cover.

IN MUTED SHADES OF CREAM AND GREY-BLUE accented with warm browns, these antique French armchairs are dressed like demure girls at a ball. The charming frills on the chair covers lend a touch of frivolity, as do the luxurious velvet trim and the flower braid on the cushions which contrast so happily with the nubbly woven linen. The woollen rug and alpaca throw emphasize the accent colours of copper and beige.

TREASURE TROVE FROM THE FLEA MARKET: a comfortable and well-shaped old armchair looks soft and relaxed covered in the calm blue and white of a tablecloth. The seat cushion is covered in equally informal ticking, and the cushion cover is simply constructed of table napkins.

Seat covers and cushions

One of the easiest and most versatile ways of adding a very personal type of decorative detail to a chair is by making up seat covers or cushions. A seat cover is an effective way to enliven a chair that has a worn rush seat or an upholstered base that has seen better days, or just to make a wooden settle or blanket box a more comfortable place to sit. Seat covers do not need to be too thick – a filling of wadding or a fairly thin foam pad will do.

The range of colours and textures that cushions can bring to a room is limited only by your imagination or budget. Cushions can be used to contrast completely with the sofa or chair they rest on, or to pick out and emphasize accent colours around the room. Very popular today are cushions made with pieces of antique embroidery, old kilims, and both *gros point* and *petit point* work. Even if you have only a treasured scrap of old tapestry, you can stitch it to a panel or border of silk, linen or velvet and trim it to make a gorgeous and very personal seat cover.

A SET OF DINING CHAIRS that are still sound and solid but whose rush seats are looking threadbare are given a completely new look with seat covers. The red four-seasons toile and smart air-force blue striped fabrics look softly elegant as scalloped skirts.

CHEERFUL SCARLET CHECKS and floral sprigs in tough cotton union make ideal seat cushions for a rustic antique settle, picking up the red of the wallpaper behind and contrasting beautifully with the green-painted finish on the furniture.

Cushion trimmings

A quick and simple way to add life and charm to a room is to jazz up your cushions. Think of each one as a little canvas on which to project some good decorative detailing ideas. Be a magpie whenever you pass a stash of antique fabrics or a remnants shop, and you will soon have assembled a stockpile of bits of lace, linen, tapestry and carpet fragments, old trimmings, fringing and buttons – the basis of your cushion-transforming kit.

If you are making a new cover from scratch, be sure you have a cushion pad to fit: they come in a good variety of shapes and sizes, feather or down ones being far preferable to foam fillings. Instead of the usual zip, experiment with closures made of linen ties or plain ribbon. Or open up a whole new area of decorative detailing with antique-button closures, or buttons used as a patterning device on the surface of the cushion.

THESE CUSHIONS IN PLAINS AND NEUTRALS can take ornate trimmings. The calm white and taupe fabrics look sumptuous but not over-fussy with their scarlet and white bobbles and tassels.

A COMPANIONABLE PAIR OF BEDROOM CUSHIONS made from checks and florals in complementary colours. The two are nicely linked by the buttons covered in checks on the flowered cushion.

Generally, the plainer the body fabric of the cushion, the more elaborate the trimmings can be. A richly embroidered or floral-patterned cushion needs only simple silk rope, piping or a contrasting backing to finish it, while a plain linen or calico cushion can be embellished with tassels, fringing, buttons and bows. A detail that works well on a plain background is the addition of a central panel or a border of interestingly patterned or textured fabric. Similarly, a delicate antique handkerchief can be stitched onto one side of the cushion and finished at the edges with a simple trimming or buttons.

Another way of adding interest to cushions is with surface decoration, such as hand embroidery (either counted-thread or free), machine embroidery, appliqué or quilting, any of which work well on cushions and can produce stylish and highly personal results.

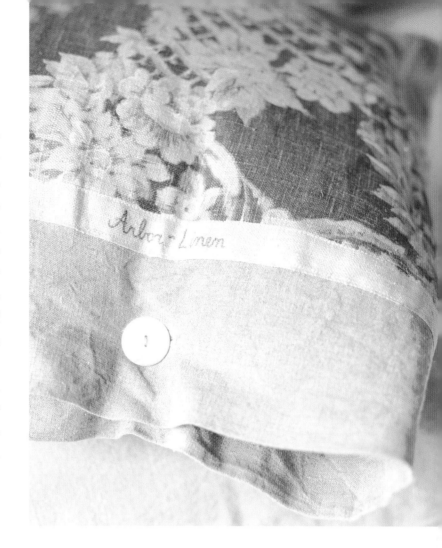

DON'T HIDE ANY ECCENTRIC LITTLE DETAILS you may find on old pieces of fabric: the writing on the selvedge of this linen adds to the charm of the cushion. Antique buttons such as this delicate incised one are easy to find and interesting to collect.

AN ANTIQUE KNITTING AND MENDING BAG has been transformed into a cushion backed with linen and fastened with matching linen ties. Decorative topstitching keeps the ties firmly in place, while the old seam is turned into a plus-point by adding a simple antique trim.

WHAT COULD BE FRESHER than this positive snowdrift of lace and cotton on a warm-toned wooden bed? The plain cherrywood four-poster looks superb draped with a lace-edged sheet as a canopy, and the antique Valenciennes and Cluny lace sheets and pillowcases take centre stage in an otherwise plain bedroom.

NATURAL, TOUCHABLE TEXTURES AND WARM COLOURS make this unpretentious bed welcoming. The browns and creams of the bedlinen and the glowing reds of the cushions and throw sit well with the bamboo table and simple garden flowers.

Traditional beds

For many centuries, the most important single piece of furniture in a house was the bed. In fact, beds belonging to aristocrats and royal personages in the last few centuries were architectural wonders with fantastic hangings. Because they were vastly expensive, they fulfilled the role of status symbol, as well as providing a place to escape the cold of a draughty castle.

In a much more moderate way, the bed is still important for people today. We spend up to a third of our lives in our beds, so they have to be comfortable, robust and beautiful. Bedrooms are the most personal and intimate rooms in the house, the places where we live our most private moments – sleep, naps, reading, letter writing, in-depth midnight talks, dressing. They are where we retreat when unwell, where we place a newborn baby when it comes home, where we think deep thoughts and make plans. And at the centre of it all is the bed. It may not be as big as the famous Elizabethan example known as the Great Bed of Ware, which is an impressive 3.3 metres (10 feet 11 inches) square – but it can be attractive and welcoming with the addition of a few cunning details.

Obviously it helps to start with a sturdy, traditional wooden bed, be it cherry, oak, walnut, maple or ash, but even a more modest bed can be dressed with inviting linens and plump pillows. Concentrate on the simpler aspects of ornamentation: you may wish to disguise a less attractive shade of wooden bed by painting it a calm, pale shade, or add a simple headboard and footboard. If the base of your bed is unattractive, hide it with a plain cotton valance. Simple cotton duvet covers and pillowcases can be customized much like cushion covers with trimmings, added borders and decorative closures (see pages 74-75 for ideas).

Metal-framed beds

After centuries of wooden beds, the first metal beds appeared around the middle of the 19th century. A typical industrial product, they were much in demand as camp beds because they could fold up so easily – even Napoleon had one on St Helena. Victorian ladies welcomed them into their homes as a hygienic alternative to the wooden frames which were unfortunately often infested with bugs. Whether their housemaids were so pleased is another matter: part of the frantic round of cleaning during that era involved taking metal beds to bits in order to wash down every part individually.

Thousands were made in countless styles, and today they are extremely popular once again, looking absolutely at home in a country setting. Also, as fashions move away from elaborate swags, tails, coronas and lavish hangings, the architectural beauty of the metal itself can come to the fore, dressed in simple linens and pale shades.

Forged iron beds are shaped by heating and hammering solid iron, whereas cast metal has rosettes of iron clamping together tubes and rods or more iron or steel. These can be finished with brass ornamentation – the famous bedknob – and a huge range of patinas and finishes: light, curling metalwork looks wonderful in flat creams and off-whites.

Another alternative is the classic brass bed, more attractive in its slightly darker and more irregularly patinated antique finish than in shiny new brass. If you are choosing an antique bed, make sure the side rails and central supports are firm and steady, for these are the real structure of the bed. Also check that a mattress is easily available in the size you have chosen: old beds do not always conform to the usual mattress measurements, and a made-to-measure mattress will turn your antique bed into a very expensive purchase.

A WONDERFULLY LIGHT AND AIRY BEDROOM, in which the open metalwork of this Portuguese iron bedstead is very much at home. The metal is painted a flat white to accentuate its pretty simplicity.

Decorative headboards

A bed in the centre of a room with no head- or footboard is said to be terrible feng shui because it makes the occupant feel decidedly vulnerable. A bed simply pushed up against a wall is also most uninviting: you feel rather like a perilously unmoored boat, about to float away at any moment. And you have nothing to lean against while reading. To feel properly contained and protected in your bed, you need at least a headboard – and preferably a footboard too, although the disadvantages for tall people are obvious.

If you have chosen a metal bed, then propped-up pillows can provide the comfort, but if you have only a bland board or something in saccharine-sweet fuchsia-pink Dralon which you would prefer not to see, then decorative details could come to your aid. Imagine your headboard as someone in dire need of a new outfit: in a boy's room, a warm travel rug or blanket could be folded over the offending headboard and tied on to achieve a hearty, masculine look. Linen sheets or old curtains folded over a layer of thick padding or even

A DRAMATIC RED LINEN COVER is embellished with diamonds cut from antique floral fabric. The palest of green braids accentuates the interesting cutaway style of the headboard.

BLUE LINEN AGAINST PALE BLUE WALLS is highlighted by pearly cream shirt buttons in a dazzling star design, framed by a frosty line of buttons around the edge. The motif needs to be sewn on quite high up so that pillows do not hide it.

antique kilims are all good sources of covering material that is strong enough for this purpose; more delicate fabrics can be appliquéd onto a heavier cover. Do make sure it is not an awkward job to remove the fabric from the headboard, as it must be able to be cleaned regularly, particularly if you have chosen a light colour. Also, keep some of the headboard fabric to use for a cushion or a throw: this can bring the look together well.

NATURALLY AT HOME IN ANY COUNTRY SETTING, an old quilt that has been used to cover a headboard is soft to relax against and beautiful to peruse at close quarters. Utilizing a damaged or remnant quilt in this way also avoids the heartbreaking task of getting rid of it. Because the headboard cover is so patterned, it is wise to keep to plain bedlinen that perhaps picks out one of the blues from the quilt.

Ties, trims and details

Beds and bedrooms lend themselves well to decorative detailing, but how do you avoid a frou-frou boudoir look while indulging your desire to add touches of ornamentation? The answer is in the variety of materials you choose to use: keep them natural, opting for solid wood or metal furnishings, cotton, linen, wool, lace or silk on the bed, and of course plenty of plants and flowers around the room to lend their scents and shades. As a general rule, avoiding anything too obviously synthetic will help. Steer your colour choices towards those gentle ones available in nature: soft pink, cream, yellow, blue, green and brown are all to be found in the herbaceous border, so bring them inside the home.

Decorative detailing that is functional as well as beautiful always has the edge. A simple satin ribbon that works as a tie-closure is somehow more satisfying

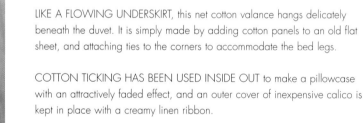

LIKE A FLOWING UNDERSKIRT, this net cotton valance hangs delicately beneath the duvet. It is simply made by adding cotton panels to an old flat sheet, and attaching ties to the corners to accommodate the bed legs.

COTTON TICKING HAS BEEN USED INSIDE OUT to make a pillowcase with an attractively faded effect, and an outer cover of inexpensive calico is kept in place with a creamy linen ribbon.

than one simply stuck on for effect, and a lining material that has a purpose but is also unexpectedly pretty is a winning touch.

Keep the frills and ruffles to a bare minimum, emphasizing instead the texture of the material, its intricate weave or pattern, or how well it falls and hangs. Highlighting the good qualities of natural materials rather than overdressing a bedroom encourages you to seek out the best of its kind in the first place, and will be gratefully received by any male occupants who, after all, must make up nearly half the world's bedroom owners.

Remember, too, how effective layers of fabric can be on a bed – a crisp white cotton piqué sheet kept in place by a good woolly blanket, with a well-worn and much loved quilt folded at the end of the bed in case of chilly nights, makes a wonderful trio of textures, patterns and colours.

RUBBER IS TOO CLAMMY AND FUR FABRIC CAN BE TICKLISH, so if you cannot live without a hot water bottle, give it a handsome cover made of a piece of old blanket or part of a woollen scarf, and finish with a simple felt motif blanket-stitched into place.

AN OLD WELSH RUG, FASTENED WITH ROBUST LEATHER TIES, turns an unexciting headboard into a warm and rugged feature. The crisp no-nonsense bedlinen is well-suited to the masculine look.

Bathroom colours

It is a bold decorator who entirely eschews the gentle tones of blue, green, cream or white for his or her bathroom. These are without doubt the firm favourites, and it is quite a shock to enter a bathroom where the decorator has taken a risk and plumped for red, orange or black.

The blues, greens, et al., are, in fact, favourites for all the right reasons – their connotations of sea, rain and tropical lagoons are appropriate in this watery environment, and the general effect of these hues is one of calm and tranquillity. And this is what is sought in a bathroom: it is a place to cleanse the mind and body, to reflect and relax. Green, blue and the neutrals provoke thought and quietude, while white is synonymous with cleanliness and purity, and so is the natural choice for baths, basins and lavatories.

Antique brass taps will lend a warm, burnished note to the room, and simple translucent curtains will allow in as much softly filtered light as possible while retaining privacy. A rural bathroom can do away with curtains completely and simply luxuriate in the open views.

BLUE WATER REFLECTS BLUE WALLS in this cool and simple room. The well-placed antique mirror throws back more light from the window, and touches of pink in the chair, bin, towel and geraniums lend warmth and contrast to the colour scheme.

TONGUE-AND-GROOVE panelling in a bathroom always lends a shipshape nautical air, especially when it is painted a clear, gentle green. The bulb pot and enamelware jug in similar sea greens continue the theme.

A DELIGHTFULLY ORIGINAL BATHROOM with primitive and ecclesiastical overtones. The walls and door are roughly colourwashed in variegated shades of yellow and cream, the towel rail is a simple piece of wood, and the scene is lit by church candles and watched over by a harp-playing angel.

Essential accessories

Just a generation or two ago, the bathroom (or the room, be it bedroom or kitchen, in which a large tin or copper bath was placed) was not generally a place to linger. Basic heating and a lack of efficient plumbing meant that rather hurried scrubs with rough flannels were the order of the day. These were ablutions that had to be performed (sometimes in tepid bathwater already used by another member of the family), rather than luxurious soaks in scented tubs.

Today, however, the art of bathing has undergone a complete makeover: plentiful hot water and central heating have transformed the way we regard this all-important room, and the fact that many homes boast more than one bathroom means it is far easier to enjoy an uninterrupted soak. Now a bath is the treat we look forward to, a reward for hard work, a reliever of stress. And if you are a devotee of the power shower rather than the bathtub, there is still a vast choice of gels and scrubs to be enjoyed.

In today's bathroom, the details and accessories are all-important to make this temple to well-being as effective as possible: capacious towel rails generously endowed with towels, soft bathrobes to dive into, a good mirror and kind lighting, relaxing or invigorating essential oils (a few drops are perfect in the water if you are not a fan of bubbles), a variety of brushes, all kinds of wonderful smelling things to pour into the bath water, a good book, and perhaps even a candle to read it by. Bath racks, which provide the perfect place to rest a book and candle, are also excellent for keeping more functional items such as soap near to hand and well-drained.

Soap is one of the most frequently bought accessories for the bathroom. It can, of course, be unromantically viewed as simply a mixture of fat, lye and water – yet the fact that such a basic recipe should, with the addition of oils and perfumes, become a cake of sweet-smelling, creamy soap is really quite magical. Buy it clear or opaque, scented or perfume-free, or make your own, adding whatever flower petals, herbs, oils or honeys you like, to create something quite unique.

FORGET BORING OLD EVERYDAY SOAP and indulge in something special: beautifully scented and tactile, the mosaic string and the ball and dice soaps flank a herbal ensemble of four rough-textured parsley, sage, rosemary and thyme soaps.

THE CLASSIC CHROME BATH RACK IS AN ESSENTIAL as well as a luxury. Supremely useful in the bath as a holding bay for body brushes, mirrors, books and cups of tea, it is also the perfect place to drain a sponge or a dripping rubber duck.

CHECK AROUND SALVAGE YARDS TO FIND TAPS and fittings ripe for reconditioning; provided they are the correct specification, they will sit well on a reclaimed bath or basin. This old spongeware bowl has found a new purpose as a cheerful soap dish.

Towels

When buying bath towels, the key word to remember is 'generous' – most bathers would agree that the towel they wrap themselves in as they step out of the bath can never be too big. Often called a bath sheet, it must envelope you from top to toe in a large and comfortable embrace. Anything that strains to cover the essentials must instantly be relegated to hand-towel status.

In any good towel, the cotton must be deeply fluffy (but not the kind of fluff that rubs off in irritating little balls) and instantly absorbent. Egyptian cotton or extra-long staple cotton is usually good, and organic cotton (which has no pesticide residue) is also available. If you prefer a smooth rather than fluffy texture for bath towels (or for hand towels) or if the weather is too warm for layers of cotton wrapped around you, try the crispness of waffle weave, or glassy white linen. (And if you buy the embroidered kind, these towels can make tremendous curtains!)

BUCKING THE TREND FOR WHITE TOWELS, this bathroom is hung with a positive citrus cocktail of zingy orange, lemon, lime and sky blue bath and swimming towels. A laundry rack fitted to the ceiling provides the ideal place for drying towels.

CRISP WAFFLE COTTON MAKES PERFECT HAND TOWELS, and the snowy whiteness of these is accentuated by the bright and simple rick-rack trimming.

A SOFT, LOOSE-WEAVE BATHROBE and traditional Swedish laundry bag hang from homely heart-shaped hooks.

Collecting and Grouping

Everyone puts together a collection at some point in their lives, even if unwittingly: a schoolboy with a few foreign coins and a little girl adding to her stack of dolls are as much collectors as the devoted philatelist. We are all imbued with certain magpie or hoarding instincts, and love to surround ourselves with objects of beauty, or interest, or sheer eccentric curiosity. Collections are as diverse as their owners, ranging from priceless works of art to plastic lunchboxes, from found objects to personal mementoes.

Collectors find that their fascination increases as their collection grows and they learn more about their chosen subject. Chinese snuff bottles, for example, may be minute, but as you collect them you will learn much about the history of the tobacco trade and about the Chinese people and their culture over the last few centuries.

Collections can look superb grouped and displayed well. They will also tell even the most casual observer a great deal about the owner and their likes and dislikes, so beware what you divulge!

Frames and framed objects

Framing is the ancient and traditional way to display an item of importance or beauty, or to bring together several such items within one frame. This artistic form of enclosure gives a special emphasis to its contents and shows them off to their best advantage. Beyond simply being highlighted, the framed item is also caught in time, preserved within its protective frame: if it is glazed, dirt and dust are kept out, and the frame back keeps it away from any cold and damp in the wall. Of course, frames need not contain only great works of art. They can look just as effective surrounding delicate scraps of antique fabric, pressed flowers and leaves, shells and stones, favourite prints or postcards, pages from a book or evocative family photographs.

For every object needing to be framed, there is the perfect frame just waiting to be found. According to tradition, the width of the frame should be between a sixth and a seventh

FORGO OLD MASTERS AND CREATE YOUR OWN WORKS OF ART: here simple pale wooden frames, some embellished with gingham, show off memories of holidays, found treasures and precious children's drawings.

of the width of the contents. Watercolours, photographs and silhouettes look good with modest frames, while those surrounding prints, oil paintings and mirrors can be larger. For the best results, choose a mount board with a bevelled-cut central aperture. The mount board can be either classic cream or a colour chosen to complement the frame or the item to be displayed.

Gilding has long been a favourite decoration on frames. To give the appearance of this precious metal, gold leaf is attached using gold size (an oil-based adhesive) in a process known as oil gilding, or using a water-based adhesive and the process of water gilding. The latter is an intricate and highly skilled technique.

The shape of the frame also has a bearing on the picture it surrounds – squares and rectangles have strong, dramatic lines, while round or oval frames create a delicate effect and suit pictures of children or miniatures. Grand scenes can take

A DELICATE PAPER-CUT from around 1800 is framed in handsome dark-stained wood with a simple line of gilding, echoing the frame of the small print above, and the elegant dining chair below.

A COLLECTION OF VICTORIAN wooden-backed hand mirrors and tortoiseshell hair combs makes a fascinating display, and has the added bonus of bringing light and sparkle into a dark corner of the room. To avoid any ugly hooks and pins showing, attach objects like this with adhesive mirror pads.

richly embellished, rococo frames. The forms found in frames are taken from a huge variety of sources. Nature provides palms, grape leaves and acanthus leaves, the sun and stars and images from the animal kingdom. Symbolism gives the frame-maker such motifs as crosses, swords, wreaths and ribbons.

With the plethora of antique and modern frames that are available, your collection could simply be of empty frames, which would look magical against a plain wall. The frames could perhaps be arranged historically, starting with early oak or pine frames (which were often painted black with just a little gilding), followed by the carved gilt frames of the 17th century onwards, and then frames made from papier mâché or 'compo' (a composition of glue, linseed oil, resin and whiting that allowed for large and elaborate frames), which were popular from the 1790s to the 19th century.

Whether hung empty as an interesting collection in themselves, or full of prints and paintings, frames must be placed and hung with care. Take into account the relationship of neighbouring frames to each other: choose whether they are centred on one another, lined up along the top of their frames, or placed in a pleasing pattern. Remember not overlook the proximity of any doors and windows, for these are all framed structures within the frame of the wall itself, and can be useful (or indeed irritating) when positioning your collection.

STRIKING HEART MOTIFS in velvet, fabric scraps and wallpaper require nothing more than pared-down frames of unpretentious design.

AN OLD LLOYD LOOM SIDE TABLE becomes a frame in itself when covered in a sheet of glass cut to size, with treasured black-and-white family photographs sandwiched between.

A SIMPLE AND HANDSOME LATE 19TH-CENTURY GILT FRAME leans casually on a mantelpiece, providing an airy and unfettered home for some antique flower prints, which are lightly tacked to the wall.

Wall displays

A collection of stunning, interesting or unusual objects grouped well and displayed for maximum impact on the wall can lift the spirits of anyone entering the room. It commands attention and can turn the simplest decor into something sublime.

Filling your home with paintings and prints can be a very expensive business, and so the walls sometimes have to wait their turn, looking rather sad and empty. But this need not be the case. With a little imagination and ingenuity, many favourite collectibles can be displayed on the walls as enchanting decorative details. Out of reach of everyday knocks and spills, the precious items are safe, and the walls of a room provide a vast blank canvas on which to play around with different groupings. Also, if your collection is copious, or made up of large and delicate items such as antique hats, storage for it elsewhere in the house can be a problem, so wall displays make a virtue out of a necessity.

Remember that if you are displaying small or intricately decorated objects, you will need to hang them at around eye level, or many of their charms will be lost. Larger, plainer items can hold their own wherever you choose to hang them, be it above a picture rail or beyond.

ANTIQUE STRAW AND FABRIC HATS provide a charmingly eccentric way to decorate a plain wall (and a very sensible way of storing them). The predominance of the pale straw colour and reds and pinks links all the disparate styles of hats and gives a satisfying cohesion to the display.

ART FOR FREE: PRESS SOME WELL-SHAPED AUTUMN LEAVES between blotting paper and heavy books for a few days, coat them with matt acrylic varnish and fix them to the wall with wallpaper paste for a delicate and enchanting decorative feature.

Porcelain and pottery

From simple earthenware to translucent porcelain, china must be one of the most popular and addictive collectibles. Obviously, the most important factor in collecting china is that you love the piece, and simply like to look at it, hold it and perhaps use it. Even if it is worth very little monetarily, it can be priceless to you for its associations and memories. If, however, you are about to spend a large sum of money on a piece of porcelain, do run your fingers over the surface to feel for bumps or roughness that may reveal cracks and repairs. 'Ping' it gently with finger and thumb – this should produce a clear ring, not a dull thud.

If you dream of a glass cabinet displaying the finest, most elegant china, then porcelain is for you. First produced in China about a thousand years ago and widely imitated in Europe during the 18th century, porcelain is made from fine white 'china' clay fired at high temperatures and highly glazed. Bone china is a distinctively English type of porcelain containing bone ash as well as china clay.

If you prefer a dresser full of more rustic tableware, hunt down cheerful pottery such as spongeware or well-used

THESE LIVELY BLUE SHELVES are crowded with a heady mixture of vibrant ceramic pieces from many eras –1920s' kitsch and Victorian and Georgian china look equally at home rubbing shoulders with a jolly spongeware jug and rustic earthenware vessels.

A FRESH AND BREEZY COMPOSITION: blue-and-white plates and platters are arranged on dresser shelves painted a toning sky blue, alongside a sailboat whose hull is picked out in the same shade.

SPONGEWARE LOOKS GOOD displayed against the rich tones of antique wood. Here, blue-and-white spongeware muffineers (muffin dishes) and table salts from around 1820 and transferware from 1800 sit comfortably with wooden 18th-century platters.

blue-and-white pieces. Ceramics that are not porcelain are classified as pottery. Pottery that is fired at a high-enough temperature to make it non-porous is known as stoneware, and all other pottery is called earthenware. Because it is fired at a comparatively low temperature, earthenware must be glazed to make it non-porous.

Pure white, undecorated pottery is becoming increasingly popular. Smooth and unpretentious creamware is an earthenware that has a buff or creamy-white body with a clear glaze. Pearlware is similar, but cobalt is included in the glaze to make the pottery seem whiter (just like a blue bag in the laundry). The pristine, restrained elegance of white ironstone, a type of stoneware, looks equally at home in a farmhouse or a contemporary apartment, and its sturdy, graceful lines make it eminently usable as everyday tableware.

THE CLASSIC BEAUTY OF CREAMWARE is well exemplified by these plates with pierced rims from 1790 and hexagonal French Monterrat plates from about a century later. Older pieces tend to be slightly darker and richer in colour, while the more modern are lighter in tone.

THE ELEGANT SIMPLICITY OF THIS GLAZED WHITE CUPBOARD makes it the perfect showcase for a collection of classic white ironstone. The shapes of the jugs, jelly moulds, bowls and dishes are easy to appreciate, with no distractions in the form of pattern or colour.

Displaying plates

Arranging your collection of plates on a wall is a great way of displaying them. Wooden plate-stands on tables or mantelpieces are too precarious for any household that contains dogs, cats or children, whereas wall-hung plates are safe from knocks and are shown off to their best advantage.

Some people hang plates using expandable plate-hangers that grip the plate around its rim, but a gentler alternative is the adhesive plate-hanger, a glued paper disk with a metal ring for hanging. Attached to the back, it not only holds the plate safely and invisibly but is easily removed and so will not affect the value of an antique.

Plates look extremely effective whether ranged in serried rows to create a serenely symmetrical pattern or dotted here and there according to size or colour. A theme looks cohesive and satisfying: colours, lettering or the illustrations themselves can be the unifying element. However, the wild eclecticism of plates you just happen to love arranged as they come has its own energetic appeal.

NO COMMON THREAD, and none the worse for it. This jazzy ensemble of very different plates is held together by the owner's individual style. In fact, the two black-and-white plates were made by the owner herself using brass rubbings from manhole covers.

PRETTY IN PALE GREEN, PINK AND WHITE, this delicate collection of plates, which includes lustreware and spongeware, successfully takes the place traditionally occupied by a painting or mirror over the fireplace.

Clear glass

Collections of glass make superb displays. They catch every ray of sun if placed in windows, they scintillate in front of mirrors and candles, and they even bring sparkle to dark corners.

Venetian glass dominated the European glass market for centuries, but the invention of lead crystal in England in 1676 led to the flowering of Anglo-Irish cut glass during the 18th and 19th centuries. When light hits the diamond-shaped facets cut in this clear and heavy glass, it is split into all the colours of the spectrum for a dazzling display. The introduction of pressed glass (made by forcing molten glass into patterned moulds) brought glass within reach of everyone from the early 1800s.

Clear glass collectibles are so diverse that the main difficulty is narrowing down the possibilities. You could choose a theme of a particular type of glassware, be it cut-glass butter dishes or engraved goblets, pressed-glass commemorative ware or unusually shaped old bottles. Alternatively, you could simply combine any shapes, sizes, periods and types of glassware that you feel look good together. Whichever approach you favour, the glass items will look better closely grouped than widely scattered.

CHARMING AND SURPRISINGLY INEXPENSIVE, this collection of British pressed glass includes water jugs, a flower trough and a small two-handled dish from the last years of the 19th century and the first quarter of the 20th.

CANDLELIGHT BRINGS OUT THE MAGIC of cut crystal and engraved glass, both vintage and modern. The antique celery vase is perfect for holding cutlery and a deep engraved vase doubles as a storm lantern.

Coloured glass

Just as stained glass transforms natural light into a sumptuous array of shades, so coloured glass collections bring their own shimmering rainbow hues into the home. A display of glassware all in one colour can look sensational.

It was the Bohemian glassmakers of the 17th, 18th and 19th centuries who were renowned for coloured glass, developing rich colours like dark blue and ruby. Coloured glass was particularly popular in Europe and America in the 19th century, and much of this is highly collectible today. Among the best-loved colours are the cobalt blues and turquoise greens known as Bristol blue and green, produced in the first half of the 19th century. Other popular colours include green, cranberry, amethyst and pink, lemon yellow and amber.

Today, craftsmen still produce exquisite hand-blown pieces using traditional techniques. So beautiful is some of this antique and modern coloured glass that you might wish to base an entire decorative scheme around a collection.

COLOURED GLASS BAUBLES set in front of a window catch the light like freshly blown soap bubbles, each modifying the shade of its neighbour, as well as the blue bowl in which the baubles sit.

ALL IN PRESSED GLASS, an amber-coloured plate from 1860 and a 1930s' green plate flank a clear celery vase. The egg-bearing trough dates from about 1880.

Books

As every bibliophile knows, a much-loved collection of books is like a crowd of old friends, one that can be visited time and time again with renewed enjoyment. Old books, especially those bound in leather or even vellum and perhaps tooled in gold, are also highly decorative and look wonderful lining a bookcase or elsewhere in a room. Don't exclude the dog-eared old favourites that show signs of frequent re-reading, or even the odd paperback or cherished childhood annual.

Books on shelves look more inviting mixed with little paintings, vases, small sculptures or other books placed horizontally to break up the regimented lines. Because the covers are often hidden when the books are standing on bookshelves, the most attractive ones could be stacked on tables beneath lights, perhaps interspersed with the odd book-related item, such as an antique bookmark or paper-cutter.

A COMFORTABLE WING CHAIR sits in readiness for a reader in front of the bookshelves. The well-thumbed paperbacks amidst the antique volumes make all feel welcome to browse.

LANDINGS ARE PERFECT
STORAGE AREAS for large
quantities of books. The informal
arranging of the books on these
closely packed shelves means
that anyone bound for bed
through the doorway will feel free
to choose some reading material.

Baskets, boxes and travel bags

The best thing about this trio of immensely decorative details is that they are also tremendously useful. Good-looking and easy to stack or hang in any room of the home, they fulfil today the purpose for which they were originally created: storage.

Wickerwork (slender, pliable twigs woven together) and basketry can be made from a variety of raw materials – rattan, rush, cane, birch bark and bamboo among them – but the most common is probably willow. You can find this in the form of traditional market baskets, picnic baskets, cradles, dog beds and planters (but these need plastic liners) in antique shops, flea markets and car-boot sales. A wonderful range of modern items can also be found in almost every high street.

Capacious Ali Baba-style wicker baskets make superb receptacles for laundry, and large wicker trunks with leather straps are useful as linen baskets. Perhaps the best and most appropriate room in the house for displaying basket collections is the kitchen. Sit baskets on the tops of wall cupboards, hang them from beams or an overhead rack, or use rattan drawers or vegetable stands. Wherever they are positioned, they will be invaluable for storage.

A HATBOX AND SUITCASE in aged tan leather hugging the foot of the bed solve storage problems in a small bedroom and preserve the spare, ordered look while adding interesting textures and shapes.

WICKER BASKETS suspended from a beam in a simple country kitchen tone well with the antique wood and blue-and-white china collection. Out of the way, they are decorative when not in use and handy when needed.

Antique suitcases have an aura of cosmopolitan glamour about them. Old leather suitcases that have crossed continents in steam trains, richly coloured carpet bags that were once stored in horse-drawn carriages, or vast cabin trunks with all their hanging and accessory space that traversed the Atlantic are instantly intriguing and charged with memories, even if not your own. Some still bear the luggage labels and stickers of travel companies and hotels long since vanished. Today, piled at the end of a bed, they are very practical places for keeping winter sweaters, extra bedding or books. Many types of travel bag can be collected, including hatboxes (still invaluable for their original purpose), Gladstone bags and medical, gun and music cases. The patina and smell of well-used leather and the gleam of brass locks and handles are perfectly at home in a country-style decor and far nicer to live with than a utilitarian cupboard.

Boxes range from tiny desk or jewellery containers in fine woods through useful finger-lapped Shaker pantry boxes to vast blanket boxes that are more pieces of furniture than accessories. But they all share an immense practicality as containers that do their job as well today as when they were made. Blanket boxes are deservedly popular: not only do they store bedding well, but the smaller ones make informal occasional tables while a long box in a bay window provides a good place to sit. Many were originally painted, and if still intact, this makes an antique box considerably more valuable.

AN ELEGANT ARRANGEMENT OF SIMILAR-COLOURED ITEMS in an uncluttered bathroom. The positioning of two curved shapes (wicker laundry basket and mirror) on one diagonal and the rectilinear chair and wall cupboard on the other create a perfect balance.

USEFUL AS A SURFACE FOR DECORATIVE ITEMS AND ALSO FOR STORAGE, this antique blanket box has attractive metal banding for added strength, and side handles for ease of carrying.

Table settings

Eating together is an important ritual. From the earliest fireside feasts through medieval banquets to today's meals with family and friends, breaking bread with one's neighbour has always been a sign of friendship and trust. It may no longer be necessary to eat from a communal bowl using our fingers, as it was in the Middle Ages, but the social ritual of sharing a meal is still important.

Making the table as welcoming to guests as possible should be a pleasure. It doesn't always have to mean ironing the best table linen, cleaning the china, polishing the silver and washing the crystal glasses. Formal dining has its place and can be extravagant fun, but informal meals and kitchen suppers are just as enjoyable. The table settings can be relaxed, diverse and imaginative, using nature's decorative details and keeping fuss to a minimum.

A TABLE OF WHITENED WOOD provides the perfect base for a delicate palette of pink and yellow china. Don't feel that pieces have to match; their very diversity can be part of the charm of an informal country lunch or breakfast.

MIX FRUIT-COLOURED NAPKINS with lemons and apricots in a plain wooden bowl. The napkins are easy to make from 50cm (20in) squares of linen, hemmed and embroidered in a simple, naive way with knots, flowers and running stitch.

Decorative table details

A good scrubbed pine table sometimes needs no cloth at all to be the perfect backdrop to your table settings. Alternatively, if you want to use a cloth but don't want to get out your best damask, an old linen sheet can be effective. Either use it plain or add subtle decorative patterning with fabric paint – a border always looks smart, and can be repeated on the napkins.

A simple white or cream cloth makes a good base for a contrasting runner down the centre: sprigged muslin or floral-patterned cotton would be ideal for a summer lunch, and tartan or rich paisley for a winter's evening. Napkins are simplicity itself to make and can match or contrast with the cloth, be a set or harlequin – you make the rules.

Never forget flowers, for they adorn and beautify any table. Keep them informal and natural, and not so high that guests have to crane over or around them to talk. If your time or your flower arranging skills are limited, bring in little terracotta pots of bay, rosemary or box plants to sit on the table, or simply arrange ivy on the cloth – the deep glossy green is unbeatable against white. Fruit in bowls looks great just as it comes, but you can add drama by frosting it with sugar or spray painting a nut or two glistening gold. Candlelight is the best for evenings. Use candles around the room and on the table for a warm and intimate atmosphere.

CRISP, UNDERSTATED ELEGANCE: a white linen napkin is folded around a single perfect bloom, and topped with a wire leaf garland bent into the guest's initial. White china and an embroidered cloth provide a perfect background.

A CASUALLY ROLLED NAPKIN Is kept in place by a rough strip of toning fabric tied around it as an instant and rather jaunty napkin ring.

Wirework and iron

The delicate tracery of wirework belies its strength, and its intricate designs seem almost at odds with its practical nature. Wirework was made in huge quantities in the late 19th and early 20th centuries, first as functional kitchenware and later as more decorative items like conservatory furniture and plant holders. Collecting wire kitchenware is fascinating – and not prohibitively expensive, because so many pieces were made. The homely day-to-day nature of plate racks, trays, trivets, whisks and egg separators makes the collector feel in touch with the original owners and users – divided wire baskets for carrying glasses and wine bottles, for example, which were made in France for the restaurant and café trade, still seem to have a whiff of Gitane about them. Once you have built up a small collection, the more structural-looking items like garlic baskets or collapsible salad shakers could be displayed on simple pale shelves or against a stark white wall for a dramatic contrast.

Cast iron or wrought iron objects make up another set of collectibles that look good in rustic, simple interiors as well as in contemporary or minimalist rooms. Their strength and elemental beauty suit pale walls and ceilings and also backgrounds of wood or brick. Wrought iron sconces or candelabra are decorative pieces that work for their living, as are sets of old cast-iron pans, hooks and herb holders.

DECORATED WITH NAIVE BIRDS AND CURLICUES, this sturdy iron herb carrier is suspended by a simple hook and can be moved to wherever it is needed.

A PRESENT-DAY WOOD AND WIRE DRAINING RACK flanks a pretty antique birdcage, below which sit a Victorian salad shaker, a diminutive basket, a plant holder and a French glass carrier. None of these items requires a huge initial outlay to start your collection, and together they make an eye-catching arrangement.

Decorative kitchen details

The kitchen is the hub of the home, and probably the place most visitors gravitate to first. Annoyingly, it is also probably the most expensive room to redo completely if you absolutely hate it. But take heart: because kitchens require so many accessories, there is great scope for adding decorative details and touches that can alter the whole look of the room.

If you are lucky and have a substantial oven, draw attention to it by surrounding it with gorgeous tiles, thereby diminishing the focus on a less attractive area of the room. Other relatively straightforward changes include a change of work surface from, say, Formica to wood or heat-resistant granite; sanding down and painting cupboard doors; adding a new sink or just changing the taps. Any of these can completely change the way you see your kitchen. More minor works are effective too – swap baggy curtains for a sheer linen

KEEP WASPS AND FLIES AWAY IN STYLE: beaded dish covers are easy to make in a plain, open-weave fabric. Hem all around, and attach beads to embroidery-thread loops caught along each edge, knotting as you go to keep all in place.

A VARIETY OF INEXPENSIVE ENAMELWARE PLATES and bowls look bright and cheerful in a kitchen. Don't worry about the odd chip or crack – these add to the charm and are testament to decades of solid work done by these hard-wearing items.

116

blind, line open shelves with eye-catching wallpaper, add a narrow lace or crochet trim to the edge of dresser shelves, or simply remove bunches of faded dried flowers or swags of dusty hops.

Kitchens inevitably need large amounts of implements, so make sure that yours are well made, decorative and suited to their purpose, down to the last simple wooden spoon and linen tea towel. You have to have a kettle, therefore choose one that is satisfying in shape. Saucepans are another necessity, but if you look out for old copper-bottomed ones and give them a clean, you can sit back and enjoy the glow. If you have a fine old chopping board or a great collection of colourful Clarice Cliff pottery, put it out proudly and hide away white plastic necessities like food processors. Take this approach throughout the room, and it will soon start to acquire the character you are searching for.

A MUCH PRIZED SET OF FIVE 1930S' ENAMELWARE SAUCEPANS and an enamelled dish look superb sitting on a matching blue-and-white checked tablecloth.

AN EFFECTIVE AND UNUSUAL DISPLAY OF KITCHENWARE: a numeral cake tin, a madeleine tin and assorted graters look surprisingly arty hanging on a plain white wall.

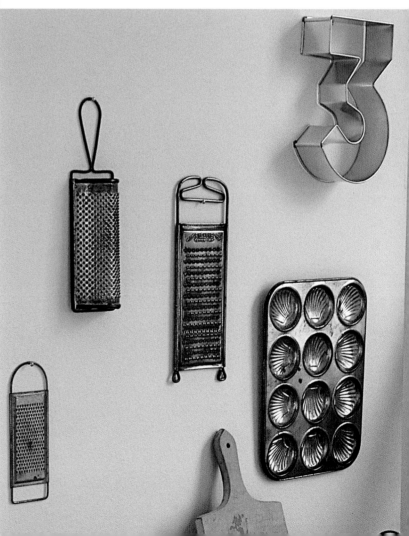

Flowers

Perhaps the most precious of decorative details, flowers bring the garden indoors, adding fragrance as well as colour, texture and form to our homes. The fleeting perfection of cut flowers is all part of their charm – like anything seasonal, from primroses to plums, we enjoy them all the more because they are soon over.

For many people, the highly structured, rigid, Oasis-bound flower arrangement is anathema – better the loose simplicity of a posy of snowdrops than the military precision of gladioli standing to attention. Trust unfettered bunches of flowers, whether wild or cultivated, to fall into their own naturally beautiful patterns, needing only the odd tweak here and there to balance the display.

The way flowers are displayed in containers is important for creating the atmosphere you want and showing them off to best advantage. Indeed, the containers are just as much part

THE PREDOMINANTLY GREEN TONES in this arrangement of roses, chrysanthemums and thistles pick up the greens of the leaves decorating the antique majolica jug in which they sit.

BEAUTY ASSEMBLED IN UNDER A MINUTE: a completely plain glass with three simple white blooms looks serene on a mantelpiece, lighting up the dark border of a brown-toned watercolour.

THE SPECKLED OCHRE, BUTTERY YELLOW AND CLAY COLOURS of this antique slipware jug, medicinal jar and confit pots perfectly complement the fresh yellow of the ranunculus and vibrant lime of the Alchemilla. In keeping with the simplicity of their container, the pots behind and the unvarnished wood table, the blooms have been allowed to fall naturally and loosely.

of the effect as the blooms themselves. Like a girl in the wrong dress, even a bunch of beautiful wild flowers can look ill at ease crammed into an inappropriate vase.

Feel free to experiment with unorthodox containers: having the freedom to use anything from a milk pail to a Lalique vase means you can tailor your flowers perfectly to their receptacles, or create some startling contrasts. Groups of terracotta pots, antique cups and jugs, or gleaming brass cachepots can work wonders in a room. They may bring to life unused summer fireplaces or dark corners, highlight favourite architectural features or even camouflage a marked surface on a much loved table.

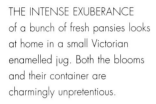

THE INTENSE EXUBERANCE of a bunch of fresh pansies looks at home in a small Victorian enamelled jug. Both the blooms and their container are charmingly unpretentious.

QUINTESSENTIALLY COTTAGE GARDEN, the perfection of curving sweet-pea stems is left unhindered in the homely blue-and-white antique transferware jug. The deep raspberry pinks and cerise of 'Snoopea' and 'Fanny Adams' seem to glow in the daylight on a window-sill.

121

Candles

Bestowing light, creating shadow, producing atmosphere, candles add a decorative touch on a formal dining table or a kitchen window-sill. They may be beautiful objects in themselves whether in the forms of fruit, pyramids, honeycomb beeswax rolls, floating wax flowers in a glass bowl of water or tall and stately white church candles. Lit and placed in the centre of a table, they create an intimacy among guests seated within the circle of illumination. Dotted along a hallway or porch, they lead guests onwards invitingly. Even a row of humble jam-jars with tea-lights tucked inside looks magical in a darkened conservatory at twilight.

To make candles work especially well as a decorative detail whether lit or unlit, make sure the container suits the candle and is good to look at in the daytime. A shimmering antique chandelier may take some restoring but looks exceptional by candlelight or daylight. Plain glass or silver candlesticks with slim white candles or weathered terracotta pots with thicker ones are equally amenable.

DECORATIVE GREEN GLASS CANDLE HOLDERS suspended by simple twisted wire look as pretty in the daytime over a country kitchen sink as they do at night casting their glowing green light.

GLOWING AMID GLOSSY BAY LEAVES, this pear-shaped candle is easy to make using a rubber mould and dye. Or customize plain candles by sticking pressed flowers and leaves to the sides, finishing with a dip in melted wax to keep the decoration in place.

THE COUNTRY GARDEN

'I have a garden of my own/ But so with roses overgrown,/ And lilies, that you would it guess/ To be a little wilderness.' The poet Andrew Marvell's garden sounds a country retreat as idyllic as the luscious tangle of cow parsley and apple blossom pictured here. Both are little wildernesses in the very best sense of the word, emphasizing seclusion, not confusion. Marvell's 'garden of my own' is his little domain, his own piece of heaven. This is what we all desire – a place where we can wander among the trees and flowers, listening to birdsong, or simply sit and reflect, and which we can also share with family and close friends.

Consider how you want to use your garden: as a private retreat, an outdoor room primarily for entertaining, a space for children's games, a productive vegetable plot or – if you have the space – a series of 'rooms' that serve all these purposes. It may be rolling lawns and flower beds merging into fields or woods, or a small urban terrace of paving and pots, but as long as it is your garden to do with as you will, you can create your own paradise.

Doors and doorways

Doors lead a curious double life. In one sense they are barriers against the outside world, and yet in another sense they provide welcoming entrances into the home or easy access from the home into the garden. And while fulfilling these functions, doors also come in an infinite variety of styles. A sturdy little cottage looks just right with thick wooden doors that protect the inhabitants from the elements and intruders, while a Regency *cottage orné* looks wonderful with delicate, glass-paned doors that let in the light and views.

Whatever style of door you choose, make sure that it is in keeping with your home. Nothing looks as depressing as a good, sound Victorian house ruined by a modern obscured plate-glass front door and flat, featureless uPVC windows; or, indeed, an innovative modern building blighted by olde-worlde oak-effect doors with fake bull's-eyes in the glass panes. If in doubt, check in your local library for the history of your area; it may show your house (or one like it) in its heyday with the kind of door it was meant to have.

The front door is a major part of the all-important first impression, and chipped paint or ill-matching door furniture does not bode well for the rest of the house. A smart coat of paint and sparkling glass, a solid door-knocker or bell and a well-shaped door-handle set you off to a flying start.

Doors from the house out to the garden can be much more casual than the front door and should allow in as much light as possible. French windows are excellent, as are stable doors, which let in sun and air while keeping animals and children firmly on one side or the other.

WIDE FRENCH WINDOWS FLUNG OPEN TO A GARDEN VIEW add to the pleasure of being in this room. Eating at the table is almost like being outside, and anyone strolling in the garden will be able to hear the piano clearly from within. The simple curtain treatment means that none of the view is lost in the daytime, but chills from the glass are minimized at night.

PERFECTLY IN KEEPING WITH THE 18TH-CENTURY COTTAGE IT ADORNS, this simple painted front door with latch is kept open to let the light from its southerly aspect stream straight into the house.

STABLE DOORS ARE IDEAL FOR KITCHENS: a certain amount of privacy and security is maintained by keeping the lower half of the door closed, while the open top lets out heat, moisture and cooking smells, and allows air to circulate.

Summer houses

Blurring the boundaries between house and garden is becoming increasingly popular, and whereas conservatories bring the garden into the house, summer houses do the reverse. Not only are summer houses a perfect decorative detail for any garden, but they also provide a very useful space for work, relaxation or straightforward hiding from the world.

The Victorians loved elaborate summer houses, with weathervanes and curly wrought-iron work, pretty tiled floors, panelled or plastered walls, fireplaces and sometimes even a cellar to hide away the tools and garden produce. Today, however, a summer house can be as simple as an old garden shed painted a soft colour, smothered in passion flower or honeysuckle, furnished with a few chairs and a table and lit only by candlelight. An unwanted outhouse – an old cowshed or dairy perhaps – could be converted, or, alternatively, a new summer house built from durable cedarwood. Installing plumbing and electricity could turn a summer house into a complete garden office (provided the approval of local planning authorities is obtained).

A CONVERTED VICTORIAN COWSHED with a few pieces of antique wooden furniture makes a wonderful retreat in which to work, read or just relax.

THIS GARDEN SHED furnished with tables and chairs is used as a studio. Cushions, pictures hung on the walls and flowers make it as inviting as a grown-up playhouse.

Hammocks and chairs

The very word hammock is evocative of comfort, leisure and summertime – lazybones sleeping in the sun. A traditional hammock strung up between two trees makes an idyllic corner in the garden even more inviting. If your corner of paradise is a treeless one, however, do not despair: just buy a hammock stand.

Consider your options from a comfort angle first when choosing a hammock. Those made from rope are classically good-looking, but you can end up imprinted with the rope pattern if you do not use a blanket, and this can be too hot sometimes. Cloth – generally canvas – was the navy's choice for hammocks in its ships, but although it is comfortable, the ventilation is not so good and the cloth is prone to rotting. Cotton string woven into a tight web is extremely flexible and cool, and works well with wooden spreader bars, or staves, to keep the tension even.

As for garden chairs, the beauty of using chairs outside is that anything goes. Luxurious steamer chairs, antique folding chairs with the patina of age, faded deckchairs, battered kitchen chairs with a lick of paint, old rattan and rush take on a rustic charm when settled in the long grass.

SET ON A WEST-FACING HILLSIDE, this collection of chairs awaits the sunset. Don't feel you have to buy a matching set of table and chairs for the garden – the eclectic mixture of plain kitchen furniture and genuine conservatory or garden chairs works well. Hanging votive candles and coloured glass lanterns will shed enough light for the party.

IF YOU HAVE ONLY ONE TREE strong enough for a hammock, there are ingenious props available to make your dream a reality. Add a drink and a good book, and you are set for a perfect afternoon.

Eating alfresco

Food and drink quite simply taste better under an open sky, which is why everyone loves a picnic. But setting up a table and chairs *en plein air* is even better, offering all the civilized comfort of a proper seat with all the perks of fresh air, flowers, butterflies, birds and bees.

Eating outside is supremely relaxing – who cares if children spill their drinks or drop their food when there is a dog or small bird to clean up after you? The crockery, glasses and cutlery you use are probably not your best, so this adds to the wonderfully casual bonhomie of the meal. The fact that the food has to travel (even if it's just out into the garden) means that simple salads, good bread, cheese and seasonal fruit are the best options. As the cook can therefore take a bit of a holiday when eating outside, a little more effort can be put into the decorative details to make the scene welcoming – wild flowers in a jug, floral cushions, crisp cotton cloths and napkins, a stripy awning. Nature can take care of the rest.

THIS JAUNTY CANVAS AWNING is suspended from inexpensive willow poles and secured with string. It is the perfect example of how an extremely simple structure coupled with some wild flowers and pretty antique tableware can lend the scene an air of celebration and *joie de vivre*.

THE FADED BLUE OF THE SLATTED GARDEN CHAIRS and antique metal chair looks wonderful against the vibrant French windows with their gingham curtains. The pale painted wicker chair and the table covered with a crochet-edged tablecloth add splashes of light to the scene. All is kept casual and relaxed, even down to the seed tray that is used for transporting tableware.

Garden tables

Just about any table looks great outside. Perhaps the one exception is something heavy in gloss polished wood, which only makes everyone anxious about knocks and spills – exactly what dining alfresco is not about. Unless the table is permanently in the garden, remember that you (and perhaps some willing helpers) will have to carry it to the perfect spot, so choose accordingly. Wicker and cane, either *au naturel* or painted in soft, pale shades, are easy to position and, being of natural plant material, look very much at home in a garden, though they cannot be left outside all the time.

Cast aluminium garden tables are extremely light, are impervious to the cold and shed rainwater well. They come in bronze, verdigris or painted finishes, often with flowery art nouveau designs incorporated in the surface, and can look romantic in a Parisian bistro kind of way. Teak is the king of outside woods and just gets better with age, while iroko hardwood is a similarly durable, handsome material for garden furniture. Mosaic-tile tables lend an aura of exotic Marrakesh, and their glorious colours look wonderful against warm brick or green grass.

However, unless you particularly want a table that will withstand the weather and stay put all year round, don't feel you have to buy specially for the garden. Any little pine kitchen table looks great laid for a supper at twilight – the secret is in the decorative detailing you add. Unexpected juxtapositions such as crisp, elegant linen on an old scrubbed butcher's block, or delicate, translucent muslin on a dark trestle table, can look particularly effective. Make sure the flowers are plentiful but not formal, and invite your guests according to the same criteria.

SNOWY WHITE TABLE LINEN LOOKS DAZZLING OUTDOORS, and by candlelight it seems to glow. Keep to a white colour scheme on your table – the flowers, fruits and blossom in the garden will provide all the other hues you need.

A JUNK-SHOP FIND HAS BEEN TURNED INTO SOMETHING RICH AND RARE. Fragments of assorted chipped and broken plates and china were fixed onto an old table top with tile adhesive, then white grout was applied between the ceramic fragments, and finally the surface was finished with a clear tile sealant.

Garden lighting

It's extraordinary how the character of a garden can change when illuminated after dark. Common shrubs and friendly herbaceous borders, lovely by daylight, are transformed into something more exotic and magical when sensitively lit after dusk. Straightforward oaks and chestnuts will reveal a majestic shadowy beauty of their own. Sources of illumination can be decorative details in their own right. Easily installed by a qualified electrician, they will make your garden come to life after dark, when all is seen – quite literally – in a new light.

Although mains-voltage electrical installations can be safely used outdoors, low-voltage electric lighting is becoming increasingly popular as it can be added to your garden with less fuss. The fittings are small and unobtrusive so they are not noticed during the day. Light levels should be kept subtly low: the effect you are after is not one of searchlight beams. Cables can be run under mulch or bark chippings, through ground-covering plants and into small channels cut in the grass and covered over. Uplights on spikes can be sunk into the ground or hidden among shrubs. Points of architectural

interest can be accentuated, paths subtly picked out with low-level diffused lights, foliage backlit and particularly fine plants spotlit. Large trees can be downlit, with lights positioned high up in the branches, or uplit against a wall to create fantastic waving shadows. Fountains, pools and waterfalls look spectacular lit from within using special waterproof fittings.

As an alternative to installing electrical cables and fittings outside, oil lamps are supremely useful and pretty, and look wonderful hung on walls or arranged on tables after dark. Lanterns of all kinds can be hooked on stands, set on top of walls or nestled in trees to illuminate dark corners.

Oil candles – durable wicks in candle oil – are versatile and charming. Choose globes of glass filled with different jewel-coloured candle oils and wicks, and suspend them from the branches of a tree (taking care that no twigs can be ignited by the flames) to create an enchanted glade with glowing candle blossoms. Frosted glass containers for oil candles look wonderful hung on shepherd's crooks and placed alongside a path to lead guests to the garden table.

A SURREAL DISPLAY OF GLOWING PAPER CARRIER BAGS, buckets and night-lights edges a mellow brick path, overhung with shadowy shrubs bearing lanterns and simple candelabra. To prevent the scene from going up in smoke, fill the paper bags with plenty of sand in which to settle your night-lights.

THE SIMPLEST LITTLE LIGHT ADDS CHARM to supper in the garden. Here, a small glass container has wire twisted around the neck, and more wire added as a carrying handle. Drop in a short ivory church candle, and hang it on the boughs of a tree with a dozen others for instant atmosphere.

Gardens by candlelight

Perhaps the most traditional and romantic way of lighting up your garden, candles come in a variety of shades and shapes, from insect-repelling citronella-scented candle bowls to garden spikes. Even unlit, their colours add vibrancy to the scene and the melted wax running down their sides is fascinatingly tactile. Add to this the almost infinite styles of container and their value as a decorative garden accessory is revealed.

The sweet naivety of nursery night-lights makes them well suited to the simplest containers, like plain glass jars, small coloured glasses, terracotta flower-pots, disks of slate and old china bowls. Clusters of night-lights, perhaps bedded in carpet moss tucked into a large tray, make wonderful points of light in the dark, like a constellation in the night sky.

Use a grand candelabrum on a plain rustic table for maximum dramatic contrast. Choose antique silver,

A SIMPLE ANTIQUE LANTERN is hung jauntily on the back of a twig chair to create just enough light for the occupant to read a book or eat supper.

THE DRAMATIC SIZZLING ORANGE OF THESE DRIPPING CANDLES hardly needs a flame. The colours are set off by the shocking pink, orange and yellow of the flower heads in a delicate wire candle-basket.

verdigris, iron or glass, and suspend light-catching glass beads and crystal drops from the arms to add to the glittering effect. Swathe the candelabrum in lengths of glossy ivy (keeping the leaves well away from the actual flames) for a centrepiece fit for a woodland feast.

Night-time breezes can be a problem for candlelit dinners alfresco, but lanterns and hurricane lamps provide the ideal solution. They come in a wonderful array of styles – etched and coloured glass, hammered and decorated tin, pierced terracotta, punched metal allowing little sparks of light to escape, and fabulous domed creations like an edifice in Red Square. They are often inexpensive and are easily found in craft shops and junk shops, so go wild and dot them all around the garden to bring drama and surprise as guests round a corner or look up into the leafy branches of a tree.

A DETAIL ASSEMBLED IN THE BLINK OF AN EYE: aluminium wire is twisted around a weathered flowerpot, ending in a heart shape with a crook to catch a nail for hanging, providing all the decoration you need when lined up along a mossy fence or around a tree trunk.

GLOWING MARMALADE HUES IN WARM TERRACOTTA, orange flowers and flames contrast marvellously with the coolness of the green leaves and the water in this pot of floating candles.

143

Planting schemes

For anyone seeking a casual, classic country garden, the title of this section must seem a complete misnomer. Surely this kind of garden simply happens by fortuitous chance as flowers self-seed, ramble and generally take over the garden? There may be an element of serendipity in any successful garden, but, in fact, the glorious cottage garden style requires quite a lot of discipline to avoid becoming a mere clashing jumble.

Serious gardeners are often led by colour schemes, plant heights and flowering seasons when planning their planting. They consider practicality when siting herb gardens near kitchen doors and beautifully scented plants like nicotiana where people sit at dusk. (Nature does sometimes take over by letting certain plants flourish in one place and expire in another, so don't try to fight this – just bow to her superior knowledge.)

Obviously, choosing traditional cottage garden plants like roses, foxgloves, hollyhocks and poppies and letting them grow in drifts and mounds sets the right tone. Planting to avoid isolated specimens that look like islands in bare earth, or regimented rows of anything (except vegetables), is also important. Nor does summer bedding that shrieks 'look at me!' in competing tones of red, pink and orange fit into this subtle scheme.

PLANTS THAT ARE GENEROUS WITH THEIR BLOOMS look perfect in the country garden. This abundantly flowered 'Albéric Barbier' rose smothers an arch with its glossy leaves and white petals, framing the view to entice one deeper into the garden.

A STARKLY STRUCTURAL WHITE BENCH is tucked into a recess in the neat box hedging to provide somewhere to sit and enjoy the veritable sea of 'Rosa Mundi'. The deep red buds of this showy wild rose open to reveal crimson flowers lavishly streaked with white.

Pots and other containers

The best decorative accessories in a garden, pots and containers allow you to bring colour and life to any part of the garden in every season. They are the lifeblood of many a small urban plot and can be used in large gardens to emphasize different features like paths, steps, gates or changes in height. Containers also offer a simple way to decorate the various 'rooms' in a garden, bringing in your own taste and imagination just as you do in the house.

Place pots in pairs to highlight an entrance or to mark the junction of paths or the boundary of a different section of the garden; set large pots containing tall plants in a line to create a screen; or fill them with white-flowered and silver-leaved varieties to brighten a dark area. Consider at what level you need the colour and scent, and then perhaps place shallow containers along the top of a wall or hang small flat-sided wall-pots filled with fragrant flowers by doors.

Choosing your pots can be difficult, simply because there are so many covetable styles and materials available. For a country style garden, you cannot fail with natural materials like stone, terracotta, wood and lead for the containers, allowing the plants to billow abundantly out. Do avoid plastic, even when it's masquerading as terracotta. It simply doesn't look as good, it doesn't age well, and it can become very brittle in the cold, cracking at the slightest tap.

Old stone urns with their pockmarked surfaces gather mosses and lichens well and over the years achieve a beautiful variegated patina. The new reconstituted or

AIRY AND ELEGANT, THIS ANTIQUE WIREWORK PLANT-STAND holds a galvanized florist's bucket of cut flowers at its summit. It even manages to make the utilitarian plant pots interesting with a contrast of lacy white on black.

PATRICIAN PUMPKIN-SHAPED URNS adorned with elegant gadroons follow the line of the path, their soft grey tones complemented by *Thymus vulgaris* 'Silver Posie', *Pelargonium* 'Madame Layal', agapanthus and verbena.

POTS FOCUS THE EYE ON THE GRACEFUL SWEEP OF A FLIGHT OF STAIRS, and the cool greens and bright whites of creeping Jennie, marguerites and alchemilla lighten what could potentially be a dark corner. The clever planter has unified the scheme by keeping to a two-colour theme of violet-blue and white in matching basket-weave terracotta pots, with a single blue pot to change the rhythm.

reconstructed stone containers – some made from stone dust, others from cast sandstone – need help to weather well and so will appreciate a dousing with live yogurt or liquid manure. On the plus side, there are hundreds of styles, from little shallow bowls to great troughs and jardinières, so you cannot fail to find something just right for your garden.

Lead containers, such as antique cisterns, are durable and often have pretty designs such as fleurs-de-lis cast on the side, but do be careful if a lead container without drainage holes is left outside in winter. If the water inside the container freezes, the lead will distort permanently.

Concrete can look much better than it sounds, but again be aware that it may soak up water into its porous surface which will crack or crumble as the water freezes and thaws, so don't leave it standing on the soil in winter.

THE VIVID CERULEAN BLUE of a Provençal glazed terracotta pot sets off the cool simplicity of these tiny white flowers, and its geometric lines provide an excellent contrast to the fragile and feathery foliage.

THESE OLD CHIMNEY POTS may not contain an abundance of blooms just yet, but their sculptural appearance makes them perfect markers for the beginning of a path leading between the hedging.

Perhaps the most beloved container of the country gardener is terracotta, whether in its natural, unglazed state or dressed in a glossy coat of ochre, green or aqua. Choose thrown pots with a myriad of decorative details like rosettes, cherubs, rustic basket-weave, crimped piecrust frills, grand gadrooning and swags, or elegant oval or rectangular moulded troughs for window-sills.

Match your plant to its pot: put a little lemon tree in a cylindrical planter patterned with the fruit; grow deep-rooting plants in classic long-toms; and put delicate trailing ivies and verbenas in wall planters depicting Apollo, Pan or the Green Man.

Don't be shy of letting form follow function by growing lilies and hostas in tall pots with flared lips to discourage slugs, or by choosing beautifully smooth terracotta forcing pots to bring your rhubarb crowns on early and keep them sweet.

A GARDEN GATEPOST BECOMES A CHEERFUL DISPLAY when hung with brightly planted galvanized buckets painted in primary-coloured stripes – much better than a bunch of balloons to attract party guests as they arrive.

A DECORATIVE METAL WIGWAM supports a honeysuckle in a gorgeously simple group of weathered terracotta flowerpots. Varying the heights and diameters in a collection of pots while keeping the style and colouring the same gives the display a sense of harmony.

Marking boundaries

The most fortunate gardeners inherit mellow stone or brick walls starred with lichen and bowed with age to encircle their own personal pleasure grounds. Beautiful in their own right, these also provide a support for plants and a barrier against pests and wind. If you have to build a new wall, use reclaimed bricks – not only will you instantly acquire a beautiful aged patina, but you will avoid the severe uniformity of machine-edged bricks with no recesses for friendly flora and fauna.

The ubiquitous larchlap fencing can be given some life with a coat of colourful paint, or reduced to a mere beast of burden by being smothered with fast-growing clematis, roses or vines. White picket fencing always looks bandbox-fresh, as does elegant wrought iron surmounting a brick wall. In a country garden you can do away with hard-edged boundaries by planting nut, yew, privet or box. To avoid breaking up a stunning open view from your garden, you could consider constructing a ha-ha (a ditch with a wall on the inner edge).

SMART AS PAINT: a white picket fence is made far more interesting by adding carved tips to the pickets, which are graduated in size from the centre outwards, so they resemble candles set into the neat green hedging.

THE PERFECT GARDEN WALL: the faded grandeur of the acorn-topped gates and mossy stones is highlighted by the fresh pink cascade of 'Zéphirine Drouhin' roses. The warmth and protection offered by a solid wall provides a sheltered environment for flourishing verbascum, alchemilla and lamb's tongue.

Paths

Some paths are purely practical: in wet weather they provide a firm surface on which to push a wheelbarrow, or allow the postman to deliver without resorting to wellingtons. These kinds of paths permit access and show the way, be it to the front door or to the compost heap. Then there are the aesthetic paths, whose main *raison d'être* is to create a beautiful pattern in the garden or to wind enticingly away, beckoning you further into a bosky glade. Yet provided the right materials are used, there is no reason why the functional type of path cannot be decorative too.

Stone slabs, for example, make paths that are both handsome and functional. York stone is perfect, but there are good imitations that weather convincingly. Bricks laid in pleasing patterns add their warm colours to any planting scheme and provide little nooks for thyme, chamomile or house leeks to grow in. For more variety, stone can be combined with brick, cobbles or pea shingle. Gravel alone is wonderful on a casual, winding path, with bordering plants cascading over the edges.

THE PERFECT APPROACH TO A PAIR OF ELEGANT IRON GATES, this all-weather path consists of a central stone walk flanked by gravel and low-level planting. The result is mellow yet neat.

AS A NARROW GRAVEL PATH passes some French windows, it is drenched in autumn sunshine and decked in the scarlet of a late-flowering *Clematis viticella*, making it as inviting as a terrace.

THE GENTLE SERPENTINE FORM of this romantic gravel path allows drifts of alchemilla and lavender to tumble over the edges like interlocking spurs on a winding river. Tall Oriental poppies and cascades of the roses 'Paul's Himalayan Musk' and 'Roseraie de l'Hay' draw the eye down the length of the curving pathway.

Garden statuary

Statues and decorative stonework bring art into the garden, just as a good painting enhances any room in the house. By dint of careful positioning, your statuary can become a superb focal point, drawing the gaze down a path or up onto the near horizon. Statuary can highlight an entrance – sentinel lions or greyhounds look marvellous flanking a gate or door – or it can punctuate a long walk: a sundial, well or dancing faun invites you to stop and gaze.

Make sure the finish is in keeping with your garden: traditional planting and architecture demand a weathered stone, lead, patinated bronze or Carrara marble, whereas concrete, multicoloured ceramic or glass-fibre will look right in a more contemporary garden. Try matching your statuary to its position – the head of Apollo on a warm south-facing wall, a bust of Dickens or Dante where you sit immersed in a good book, or Beethoven's furrowed brow gazing down on the summer house where violin practice takes place. As with new pots that need a little instant ageing, a good coating of either live yogurt or liquid manure will quickly promote a nicely weathered look on any new statuary, and with the minimum of encouragement ivy will grow generously over its contours.

ALTHOUGH MANY EXAMPLES OF OLD STATUARY are highly valuable, you can still stumble on bargains. This little nymph was nothing special when purchased cheaply in a street market, but a few winters and summers, the odd yogurt face-pack and a trailing mantle of ivy have transformed her into a mysterious and decorative addition to the garden.

AN ANTIQUE TERRACOTTA STATUE OF ST MARTIN produces an atmosphere conducive to contemplation in a quiet corner of a garden, and the stillness of the statuary provides an interesting contrast with the moving, living plants.

ALL THE RAGE IN THE ERA OF THE GRAND TOUR, Italian statuary (or copies of it) has peppered many an English garden for centuries. This noble-profiled Aphrodite is a copy of the Florentine original.

Bird tables and nest boxes

Nesting boxes and feeding tables for the birds in your garden have a pretty straightforward job to do, but they need not be uninspiring lumps of wood or ugly plastic containers. Most gardeners would rather have a positively pleasing decorative addition to the garden, so long as it does the job just as well. If you make and site the box or table correctly, the odd little bit of woodcarving or decorative detailing will not put off any prospective avian visitor.

A nest box must be made from wood sturdy enough to withstand the weather and should be finished in a non-toxic paint or preservative – never creosote. Make sure you place it at least 1.2 metres (4 feet) off the ground, with a good, clear flight path to the entrance. It should face north, north-east or south-east and never be sited in direct sunlight. Remember that different birds like quite dissimilar homes: owls prefer chimney-shaped structures, finches like small entrances to their boxes, robins and wrens prefer open-fronted boxes tucked behind ivy or hedging, and house martins particularly like little moulded bowls mimicking their own nests tucked under the eaves.

Although it may seem a good idea to erect a bird table near the nest box, rather like providing the birds with room service, in reality the hubbub of the noisy crowd feeding at the table would be unwelcome to a quiet nesting bird, and your box would probably remain uninhabited.

Free-standing tables can have attractive roofs to discourage large birds, or a mesh surround to make them squirrel- and starling-proof. Don't be seduced by rustic knobbly poles for your bird table. This makes life much too easy for the local cats, so go for smooth and slippery every time. Unsalted peanuts, soaked bread, boiled rice, short pieces of bacon rind, fat, seed cake and sunflower seeds will all be most welcome, and your regular visitors will pay you back with their liveliness, beauty and gratifying ability to consume large amounts of greenfly and snails.

SEEDS AND PEANUTS fill the indentations of an old baking tray fixed to a pole, creating an instant and inexpensive bird table.

HOLES HAVE BEEN DRILLED IN THIS LOG and filled with seeds and bird cake. Antique chains are fixed to the ends, and the log suspended from a tree to make a bird table that blends in completely with the garden. Seeds and nuts can also simply be pushed in tree trunk crevices, and fat smeared on the bark as a feast for treecreepers.

AN IDEAL HOME and a positive pleasure to behold, this traditionally shaped nest box has been painted in subtle complementary shades and embellished with a simple twist of wood to give it great charm.

Index

Photographic Acknowledgments

Caroline Arber pages 7, 24, 30, 31, 58 (right), 61, 80 (left), 88, 92, 93, 97, 99, 117 (right), 136, 143 (right), 146 (top)

Jan Baldwin pages 34, 87

Simon Brown page 122

Charlie Colmer pages 23 (right), 35, 60, 98, 129, 130, 131 (bottom), 142 (right), 149 (left)

Harry Cory Wright pages 116 (right), 117 (left), 135

Christopher Drake pages 32, 51, 53 (left), 69, 76, 78 (bottom), 79, 87-88, 89 (left), 95 (right)

Polly Eltes page 75 (right)

Craig Fordham page 70

Kate Gadsby pages 90 (top), 139, 146 (bottom)

Catherine Gratwicke page 115

Melvin Grey page 15

Huntley Hedworth pages 12-13, 29, 36, 40, 105, 106, 131 (top), 133, 144, 153 (top)

Richard Holt pages 140, 142 (left), 143 (left)

Sandra Lane pages 100, 102

Francine Lawrence page 155 (left)

Tom Leighton pages 52 (left), 63, 64, 72 (left), 72 (right), 73, 75 (left), 113, 137, 154

Simon McBride page 26

James Merrell pages 16, 17, 18 (right), 19 (right), 25, 27, 41, 44-45, 47, 49, 50, 52 (right), 53 (right), 54, 57, 59, 62, 65, 66 (left), 67 (left), 67 (right), 68, 74 (left), 74 (right), 80 (right), 81, 95 (left), 103, 104, 114, 119, 123, 147, 148 (right)

Tham Nhu Tran pages 101, 112

David Parmiter page 48

Debbie Patterson page 55

Clay Perry pages 126-127, 151, 153 (bottom)

Nick Pope pages 111, 116 (left), 134, 141

Alex Ramsay pages 8, 28, 37 (top), 38, 94, 108, 132, 148 (left), 152

Trevor Richards page 76 (left)

Stephen Robson pages 144, 150, 155 (right)

Ron Sutherland pages 77 (right), 109

Debi Treloar pages 1, 18 (left), 19 (left), 22, 23 (left), 37 (bottom), 58 (left), 90 (bottom), 107, 110, 118 (left)

Pia Tryde pages 2, 3-4, 39, 66 (right), 78 (top), 89 (right), 96, 118 (right), 120, 121, 138, 149 (right), 156 (top), 156 (bottom), 157

Peter Wolosynski page 21

Polly Wreford page 91

Styling by Carl Braganza, Sarah Bratby, Katrin Cargill, Nicola Goodwin, Tanya Goodwin, Jayne Keeley, Ben Kendrick, Mary Norden, Hester Page, Kristin Perers, Pippa Rimmer and Gabi Tubbs

Addresses and Resources

The shops and companies listed here provide a wide range of items similar to those featured in the photographs in this book.

ANTIQUES MARKETS

Alfie's Antique Market
(Tuesday to Saturday)
13-25 Church Street
London NW8 8DT
Tel: 020 7723 6066

Antique Forum
(Fridays)
The Corn Hall
Cirencester
Gloucestershire
Tel: 01225 765586

Antiques and Collectors' Fair
(Six times a year at weekends)
Royal Bath and West
  Showground
Shepton Mallet
Somerset
Tel: 01636 702326
www.dmgantiquefairs.com

Antiques and Collectors' Fair
(Bimonthly)
Newark and Nottingham
  Showground
Newark
Nottinghamshire
Tel: 01636 702326
www.dmgantiquefairs.com

Antiques and Collectors' Market
(Seven times a year)
Goodwood Racecourse
Chichester
West Sussex
Tel: 01243 755022
www.gloriousgoodwood.co.uk

Bermondsey Antiques Market
(Friday mornings)
Bermondsey
London SE1
Tel: 020 7351 5353

Camden Passage Antiques Market
(Wednesday and Saturday mornings)
Camden Passage
London N1
Tel: 020 7359 0190

Pierce Hall Flea Market
(Thursdays)
Halifax
West Yorkshire
Tel: 01422 321002/358087

Portobello Road Market
(Friday and Saturday)
Portobello Road
London W11
Tel: 020 7341 5277
www.portobelloroad.co.uk

Samlesbury Hall Antique Market
(Tuesday to Sunday)
Preston New Road
Samlesbury
Preston
Lancashire
Tel: 01254 812010

ANTIQUE RESTORATION AND BUILDING CONSERVATION

The Building Centre
26 Store Street
London WC1E 7BT
Tel: 020 7692 4000
www.buildingcentre.co.uk

English Heritage
23 Savile Row
London W1S 2ET
Tel: 020 7973 3000
www.english-heritage.org.uk

European Reclamation & Historic Tile Co
4524 Brazil Street
Los Angeles CA 90039
USA
Tel: 848 241 2152
For nearest retailer, phone 818 547 4247
www.historictile.com

The Georgian Group
6 Fitzroy Square
London W1T 5DX
Tel: 020 7387 1720

The Victorian Society
1 Priory Gardens
London W4 1TT
Tel: 020 8994 1019
www.victorian-society.org.uk

W J Cook and Sons
(Antique restorers)
High Trees House
Savernake Forest
Marlborough
Wiltshire SN8 4NE
Tel: 01672 513017

ARCHITECTURAL MOULDINGS

Homebase
Tel: 0870 900 8098 for branches
www.homebase.co.uk

London Architectural Salvage Company
St Michael's Church
Mark Street (off Paul Street)
London EC2A 4ER
Tel: 020 7749 9944

Salvo
(Architectural reclamation listings magazine)
PO Box 333
Cornhill on Tweed
Northumberland TD12 4YJ
Tel: 01890 820333
www.salvo.co.uk

Walcot Reclamation
The Depot
Riverside Business Park
Lower Bristol Road
Bath BA2 3DW
Tel: 01225 335532
www.walcot.com

BATHROOM FURNITURE AND ACCESSORIES

Bed and Bath Elegance
3801 50th Street
Suite 2
Lubbock TX 79413
USA
Tel: 806 797 5655
Toll-free orders: 800 307 7054
www.bedandbathelegance.com

The Celtic Herbal Company
(Soaps)
Baldwins Moor
Manorbier
Nr Tenby
Pembrokeshire SA70 7TY
Tel: 01834 871312

The Continental Linen Company
(Towels and robes)
The Hall Wing
Ashby St Mary
Norwich
Norfolk NR14 7BJ
Tel: 01508 480991

C P Hart
(Bathroom fittings)
Noonham Terrace
Hercules Road
London SE1
Tel: 020 7902 1000

Diana Drummond Limited
(Soaps, lotions, etc)
Arichastlich
Glen Orchy
By Dalmally
Argyll PA33 1BD
Tel: 01838 200450
www.dianadrummond.com

Fizzy Warren Decorative Antiques and Jane Benson Antique Eyes
(Wooden brushes)
The High Street
Stockbridge
Hampshire SO20 6EY
Tel: 01264 811137

Knots Elementals
(Essential oils, etc)
29 St James's Avenue
Hampton Hill
Middlesex TW12 1HH
Tel: 020 8941 0759

Lloyd Loom of Spalding
(Traditional Lloyd Loom
furniture)
Wardentree Lane
Pinchbeck
Spalding
Lincolnshire PE11 3SY
Tel: 01775 712111
www.lloydloom.com

Neal's Yard Remedies
(Essential oils)
29 John Dalton Street
Manchester M2 6DS
Tel: 0161 831 7875
www.nealsyardremedies.com

Potions and Possibilities
(Handmade soaps, etc)
The Old Forge
Bredfield
Woodbridge
Suffolk IP13 6AE
Tel: 01394 386161
www.potions.co.uk

Ronsons Reclamation
Norton Barns
Wainlodes Lane
Gloucester GL2 9LN
Tel: 01452 731236

Victorian Bathrooms
Ings Mill
Dale Street
Ossett
Wakefield WF5 9HQ
Tel: 01924 267736
www.victorianbathrooms.co.uk

Walcot Reclamation
108 Walcot Street
Bath BA1 5BG
Tel: 01225 444404
www.walcot.com

BEDS AND BEDROOM ACCESSORIES

Antique Bed Shop
Napier House
Head Street
Halstead
Essex CO9 2BT
Tel: 01787 477346

Avoca Handweavers
Avoca
Locations around Ireland
Tel: 353 1 286 7466 for
branches
www.avoca.ie

Catheryn Huntly
(Cushions and quilts)
Aboyne Castle
Aberdeenshire AB34 5JP
Tel: 01339 887061
www.catherynhuntly.co.uk

Cottonwood
8 Main Street
Dundrum
Dublin 14
Tel: 01 298 9599

Dyvig Metalwork Design
2 Mill Street
Brightlingsea
Colchester
Essex CO7 0EJ
Tel: 01206 824466

Guinevere
(Antique bedlinen)
574-580 King's Road
London SW6 2DY
Tel: 020 7736 2917

The Iron Bed Company
Funtington Park
Funtington
Chichester
West Sussex PO18 8UE
Tel: 01243 578888
www.ironbed.co.uk

The Linen Source
PO Box 31151
Tampa FL 33631
USA
Tel: 800 434 9812
www.linensource.com

Monogrammed Linen Shop
168 and 184 Walton Street
London SW3 2JL
Tel: 020 7589 4033
www.monogrammed
linenshop.co.uk

The Odd Mattress Factory
(Unusual sized mattresses)
Cumeragh Lane
Whittingham
Preston
Lancashire PR3 2AL
Tel: 01772 786666

Seventh Heaven
(Antique bedsteads)
Chirk Mill
Chirk
Wrexham LL14 5BU
Tel: 01691 777622
www.seventh-heaven.co.uk

Victorian Brass Bedstead Company
Hoe Copse
Cocking
Nr Midhurst
West Sussex GU29 0HL
Tel: 01730 812287

The White Company
(Bedlinen)
Perivale Industrial Park
Horsenden Lane South
Greenford
Middlesex UB6 7RJ
Tel: 08701 601610
www.thewhitecompany.co.uk

BOXES, BASKETS AND SUITCASES

An Angel at My Table
14 High Street
Saffron Walden
Essex CB10 1AY
Tel: 01799 528777

Dolly's Boathouse
(Willow lobster pots)
The Old Custom House
Wharf Road
St Ives
Cornwall TR26 1LF
Tel: 01736 796080
www.dollysboathouse.com

Hold Everything!
Cherry Creek
3000 E. First Avenue
Suite 253
Denver CO 80206
USA
Tel: 800 421 2264
www.holdeverything.com

The Holding Company
241-245 Kings Road
London SW3 5EL
Tel: 020 7352 1600
and
41 Spring Gardens
Manchester M2 2BG
Tel: 0161 834 3400
Tel: 020 7610 9160 for mail
order
www.theholdingcompany.co.uk

Shaw to Shore
(Vintage luggage)
Paulk Mill House
Offenham
Evesham
Worcestershire WR11 5RH
Tel: 01386 424331

Tobias and The Angel
68 White Hart Lane
London SW13 0PZ
Tel: 020 8878 8902

CHINA AND CERAMICS

Marisa Arna
(Contemporary ceramics)
High Street
Thorpe-Le-Soken
Essex CO16 OEA
Tel: 01255 862355
www.marisaarna.co.uk

The Cat and the Moon
4 Castle St.
Sligo
Tel: 071 43686

China and Glass Quarterly Magazine
www.oaklandpublications.com

The China Detectives
(Matching service)
PO Box 3931
Wareham
Dorset BH20 6YD
Tel: 01202 620466
www.chinadetectives.
freeserve.co.uk

Chinasearch
(Matching service)
PO Box 1202
Kenilworth
Warwickshire CV8 2WW
Tel: 01926 512402
www.chinasearch.uk.com

Clarice Cliff Collectors' Club
Fantasque House
Tennis Drive
The Park
Nottingham NG7 1AE
www.claricecliff.com

Country Traditionals
(Blue and white Polish Bunzlau ceramics)
15 St Christopher's Place
London
W1M 5HD
Tel: 01342 822622
www.countrytraditionals.com

Deliverance County
(Household ceramics)
25 High Street East
Uppingham
Rutland LE15 9PZ
Tel: 01572 820080

Emma Bridgewater
(Spongeware)
739 Fulham Road
London SW6 5UL
Tel: 020 7371 5264
www.bridgewater-pottery.co.uk

George & George
(Contemporary ceramics)
Hookwood Cottage
Puttenden Road
Shipbourne
Tonbridge
Kent TN11 9RJ
Tel: 01732 810636

Kiltrea Bridge Pottery
Kiltrea
Enniscorthy
Co. Wexford
Tel: 054 35107

Lovers of Blue and White
(Blue and white china collectors information)
Steeple Morden
Royston
Hertfordshire SG8 0RN
Tel: 01763 853800
www.blueandwhite.com

Nicholas Mosse Pottery
Bennetsbridge
Co. Kilkenny
Tel: 056 27105

Pier 1
461 5th Avenue
New York NY 10017
USA
Tel: 212 447 1610
Tel: 800 447 4371 for stores nationwide
Tel: 800 245 4595 for customer services
www.pier1.com

Pottery Barn
1965 Broadway
New York NY 10012
USA
Tel: 800 922 5507 for stores nationwide
www.potterybarn.com

Replacements Ltd
(China matching service)
1089 Knox Road (showroom)
PO Box 26029
Department 7
Greensboro NC 27420
USA
Tel: 1 800 737 5223
www.replacements.com

Tobias and The Angel
(Antique ceramics and china)
68 White Hart Lane
London SW13 0PZ
Tel: 020 8878 8902

CURTAINS

Appeal Conservatory Blinds
6 Vale Lane
Bedminster
Bristol BS3 5SD
Tel: 0800 975 5757
www.appeal-blinds.co.uk

The Blind Wizard
5264 N University Drive
Lauderhill FL 33351
USA
Tel: 954 741 0671 and
561 278 9981
www.blindwizard.com

The Curtain Exchange
(Second-hand curtains)
Tel: 020 7731 8316 for branches
www.thecurtainexchange.net

Morris Country Interiors
(Handpainted curtain poles and hold-backs)
Anglo Trading Estate
Shepton Mallet
Somerset BA4 5BY
Tel: 01749 342769

Sheer Ideas
(Panels and fabrics in voile, muslin, etc)
Shakespeare Way
Whitchurch Business Park
Whitchurch
Shropshire SY13 1LJ
Tel: 0870 600 6070

Wholesale Window Treatments
147 Stockton Lane
Marlton NJ
USA
Tel: 800 808 5700
www.wwtc.com

FABRICS

Cath Kidston
8 Clarendon Cross
London W11 4AP
Tel: 020 7221 4000
www.cathkidston.co.uk

Designers Guild
267 King's Road
London SW3 5EN
Tel: 020 7243 7300
www.designersguild.com
and
c/o Osborne & Little
979 Third Avenue
Suite 520
New York NY 10022
USA
Tel: 212 751 3333

Ian Mankin
109 Regents Park Road
Primrose Hill
London NW1 8UR
Tel: 020 7722 0997

Jane Churchill
151 Sloane Street
London SW1X 9BX
Tel: 020 7730 9847

Lee Jofa
Knighton Heath Industrial
  Estate
851 Ringwood Road
Bournemouth BH11 8NE
Tel: 01202 575457
and
201 Central Avenue South
Bethpage NY 11714
USA
Tel: 516 752 7600 and
800 453 3563
www.leejofa.com

The Natural Fabric Company
Wessex Place
127 High Street
Hungerford
Berkshire RG17 0DL
Tel: 01488 684002

Osborne & Little
49 Temperley Road
London SW12 8QE
Tel: 020 8675 2255
www.osborneandlittle.com
and
979 Third Avenue
Suite 520
New York NY 10022
USA
Tel: 212 751 3333

Pierre Frey
251-253 Fulham Road
London SW3 6HY
Tel: 020 7376 5599
www.pierrefrey.com

Vintage Textiles
24000 Robinson Canyon Road
Carmel Valley CA 93923
USA
Tel: 831 625 6655
www.vintagetextiles.com

Yves Delorme
Tel: 01296 610212 for outlets
www.yvesdelorme.com

FLOORING MATERIALS

**The Alternative Flooring
Company**
14 Anton Trading Estate
Andover
Hampshire SP10 3RU
Tel: 01264 335111
www.alternative-flooring.co.uk

Crucial Trading
PO Box 11
Duke Place
Kidderminster
Worcestershire DY10 2JR
Tel: 01562 825656
www.crucial-trading.com

Fired Earth
Twyford Mill
Oxford Road
Adderbury
Banbury
Oxfordshire OX17 3HP
Tel: 01295 814399
(stores nationwide)
www.firedearth.com

Forbo-Nairn
PO Box 1
Kirkaldy
Fife KY1 2SB
Tel: 01592 643777
www.forbo-nairn.co.uk

**Hardwood Manufacturers
Association**
400 Penn Center Boulevard
Suite 530
Pittsburgh PA 15235
USA
www.hardwood.org

Natural Carpets Ltd
Talent House
Charlton
Hampshire SO10 4AX
Tel: 01264 336845

Natural Flooring Direct
46 Webbs Road
London SW11 6SF
Tel: 0800 454721

**The Natural Wood Floor
Company**
20 Smugglers Way
London SW18 1EQ
Tel: 020 8871 9771
www.naturalwoodfloor.co.uk

The Persian Carpet Studio
The Old White Hart
Long Melford
Sudbury
Suffolk CO10 9HX
Tel: 01787 882214
www.persian-carpet-studio.net

Roger Oates Design
(Rugs, runners, etc)
1 Munro Terrace
London SW10 0DL
Tel: 020 7351 2288
www.rogeroates.com

Wicander
(Cork and wood floors)
Amorim House
Star Road
Partridge Green
Horsham
West Sussex RH13 8RA
Tel: 01403 710002
www.amorim.com

The Wood Floor Centre
3 Whitehall Road
Aberdeen AB25 2PP
Tel: 01224 647744

FRAMES

Alastair Milne
249-251 Kensall Road
London W10 5DB
Tel: 020 8968 6807

Artists Framing Warehouse
3247 NW 29th Avenue
Portland OR 97210
USA
Tel: 800 675 1477
www.artistsframing.com

Bel Frames
56 Longfield Avenue
Mill Hill
London NW7 2EG
Tel: 020 8203 7477

The Framing Guild
104 W Jefferson Street
Falls Church VA 22046
USA
Tel: 703 533 8855
www.framingguild.com

Sue Rawley Repoussé Artist
72 Waterside Centre
Trumpers Way
London W7 2QD
Tel: 020 8992 4263
www.suerawley.co.uk

GARDEN ACCESSORIES

Alpine Lodge Company
(Garden offices)
The Farmyard
Colston Lane
Harby
Leicestershire LE14 4BE
Tel: 01949 860482
www.alpinelodge.co.uk

The Arboretum
Kilkenny Road
Rathvinden
Leighlinbridge
Co. Carlow
Tel: 0503 21558
www.arboretum.ie

Arizona Pottery
(Terracotta pots)
Arizona
USA
Tel: 480 314 0273
www.arizonapottery.com

Bailey's Home and Garden
The Engine Shed
Station Approach
Ross-on-Wye
Herefordshire HR9 7BW
Tel: 01989 563015
www.baileyshomeandgarden.
com

Carpenter Oak and Woodland Co Ltd
(Oak framed structures)
Hall Farm
Thickwood Lane
Colerne
Chippenham
Wiltshire SN14 8BE
Tel: 01225 743089
www.carpenteroak.co.uk

The Cottage Garden Society
244 Edleston Road
Crewe
Cheshire CW2 7EJ
Tel: 01270 250776
www.alfresco.demon.co.uk

Crawford Direct Ltd
(Hammock-style chairs)
Crawford House
Coldridge
Crediton
Devon EX17 6AT
Tel: 01392 668008
www.crawford-direct.co.uk

C J Wildbird Foods
The Rea
Upton Magna
Shrewsbury
Shropshire SY4 4UR
Tel: 01743 709545
0800 731 820
www.birdfood.co.uk

Kootensaw Dovecotes
Oakwood
Cider Works
Chudleigh
Newton Abbot
Devon TQ13 0EL
Tel: 01626 854999
www.dovecotes.co.uk

Fallen Fruits
(Garden accessories)
The Potting Shed
Richards Castle
Ludlow
Shropshire SY8 4DS
Tel: 01584 837377

Garden Images Ltd
(Accessories)
Highfield House
Wavensmere Road
Solihull
West Midlands B95 6BN
Tel: 01564 794035
www.garden-images.co.uk

The Garden Shop
(Furniture and accessories)
PO Box 1364
Chippenham
Wiltshire SN15 3HZ
Tel: 01249 656467

Graeme Mitcheson Stone Carving
(Sculptures)
The Ferrers Centre
Staunton Harold
Ashby
Leicestershire LE65 1RU
Tel: 01332 865639
www.chisel-it.co.uk

Haddonstone
(Garden statuary and pots)
The Forge House
Church Lane
East Haddon
Northamptonshire NN6 8DB
Tel: 01604 770711
www.haddonstone.co.uk

Homestead Timber Buildings
Wyndham House
Lupton Road
Wallingford
Oxfordshire OX10 9TD
Tel: 01491 839379
www.homesteadtimberbuildings
.co.uk

Ironart of Bath
(Garden furniture)
Upper Lambridge Street
Larkhall
Bath BA1 6RY
Tel: 01225 311273

Jane Hogben Terracotta Pots
Grove House
East Common
Gerrards Cross
Buckinghamshire SL9 7AF
Tel: 01753 882364
www.janehogbenterracotta.co.uk

LL Bean Inc (USA)
Freeport ME 04033-0001
Tel: 800 441 5713 for customer
services and orders
www.llbean.com

Nomad Design
(Garden art)
Union Hall
27-29 Union Street
London SE11 1SD
Tel: 020 7978 9985
www.nomad-design.co.uk

Outside Edge
(Mosaic tables)
Rooksmoor Mills
Bath Road
Woodchester
Nr Stroud
Gloucestershire Gl5 5ND
Tel: 01453 835940

Phillips Follies
Hole House Lane
Glue Hill
Sturminster Newton
Dorset DT10 2AA
Tel: 01258 472846
www.englandjoinery.co.uk

The Pot Shop
Violet Cottage
Upper Sapey
Worcester WR6 6XT
Tel: 01886 853206

The Potting Shed
(Antique garden paraphernalia)
13 London Road
Alderley Edge
Cheshire SK9 7JT
Tel: 01625 585819

Room in the Garden
(Iron edifices)
Oak Cottage
Furzen Lane
Ellens Green
Rudgwick
West Sussex RH12 3AR
Tel: 01403 823958

GLASS

Crate & Barrel (USA)
Tel: 800 967 6696 for locations
www.crateandbarrel.com

The Dining Room Shop
62-64 White Hart Lane
London SW13 0PZ
Tel: 020 8878 1020

Lara Aldridge Glass
16 Turner Dumbrell Workshops
North End
Ditchling
East Sussex BN6 8TD
Tel: 01273 844550
www.lara-aldridge.com

The Pressed Glass Collectors' Club
4 Bowshot Close
Castle Bromwich
West Midlands B36 9UH
Tel: 0121 681 4872
www.pressedglasscollectorsclub.
pwp.blueyonder.co.uk

Summerill & Bishop
(Pressed glass)
100 Portland Road
London W11 4LN
Tel: 020 7221 4566

William Yeoward Cut Glass
336 King's Road
London SW3 5UR
Tel: 020 7351 5454
www.williamyeowardcrystal.com

KITCHEN ACCESSORIES

An Angel at My Table
(Enamel, glassware, etc)
14 High Street
Saffron Walden
Essex CB10 1AY
Tel: 01799 528777

Ann Lingard Antiques
(Utility/vintage kitchen accessories)
18-22 Rope Walk
Rye
East Sussex TN31 7NA
Tel: 01797 223486

Anne Fowler
(Wirework)
35 Long Street
Tetbury
Gloucestershire GL8 8AA
Tel: 01666 504043

Barker's
36-40 South Main Street
Wexford
Tel: 053 23159

Celestino Valenti Wireworks
Brewery Arts
Brewery Court
Cirencester
Gloucestershire GL7 1JH
Tel: 01285 657622
www.glosarts.co.uk

Crate & Barrel
650 Madison Avenue
New York NY 10022
USA
Tel: 212 294 0011
Tel: 800 967 6696 for stores nationwide
www.crateandbarrel.com

Culinary Concepts
(Tablewares)
Unit 29
Cannon Wharf Business Centre
35 Evelyn Street
London SE8 5RT
Tel: 08702 411689
www.culinaryconcepts.co.uk

Dean & Deluca
560 Broadway
New York NY 10012
USA
Tel: 212 226 6800
Mail order: 800 221 7714 or 800 999 0306
www.deandeluca.com

The Design Concourse
Merchant's Houe
Kirwan's Lane
Cross Street
Galway
Tel: 091 566 016

Divertimenti
139–141 Fulham Road
London SW3 6SD
Tel: 020 7581 8065
www.divertimenti.co.uk

Just Doors
(Kitchen cupboard replacements)
Grove Technology Park
Downsview Road
Wantage
Oxfordshire OX12 9FA
Tel: 0870 200 1010
www.justdoors.co.uk

Kitchen Bygones
Stand BO51-53
Alfie's Antique Market
13-25 Church Street
London NW8 8DT
Tel: 020 7723 6066

Knobbs Hardware
(Door and cupboard knobs)
Quarter Cefn
Maenclochog
Clynderwen
Pembrokeshire SA66 7LH
Tel: 01437 532587
www.door-knobs.co.uk

My House
(Tartan kitchenware)
126 St Stephen Street
Edinburgh EH3 5AD
Tel: 0131 622 7272

Myriad Antiques
(Wirework)
131 Portland Road
London W11 4LW
Tel: 020 7229 1709

Pier 1
461 5th Avenue
New York NY 10017
USA
Tel: 212 447 1610
Tel: 800 447 4371 for stores nationwide
www.pier1.com

Pottery Barn
1965 Broadway
New York NY 10023
USA
Tel: 800 922 5507 for stores nationwide
www.potterybarn.com

Rayment Wireworks
Unit 7
Hoo Farm Industrial Estate
Monkton Road
Minster in Thanet
Kent CT12 4JB
Tel: 01843 821628
www.raymentwire.co.uk

Stephen Pearce Pottery
Shanagarry
Co. Cork
Tel: 021 464 6807

Trevor Mottram Copper Moulds
33-37 The Pantiles
Tunbridge Wells
Kent TN2 5TE
Tel: 01892 538915

Williams-Sonoma (USA)
Tel: 800 541 2233 for stores
www.williams-sonoma.com

LIGHTING AND CANDLES

Candleberry
25 Westbury Mall
Dublin 2
Tel: 01 671 8441

Candlemakers Supplies
28 Blythe Road
London W14 0HA
Tel: 020 7602 4031

Christopher Wray
591–593 Kings Road
London SW6 2YW
Tel: 020 7751 8701
www.christopher-wray.com

Delusions of Grandeur
(Chandeliers)
1 Lime Villas
High Street
Elham
Canterbury
Kent CT4 6TA
Tel: 01227 765922

Jane Knapp Wall Lights
6 Chatham Row
Bath BA1 5BS
Tel: 01225 463468

The Natural Light Co
(Botanical candles)
North Field Farm
Great Lane
Clophill
Bedfordshire MK45 4DD
Tel: 01234 381801
www.naturallight.co.uk

Olivers Lighting Company
Udimore Workshops
Udimore
Rye
East Sussex TN31 6AS
Tel: 01797 225166

Regali
(Table lamps, sconces, etc)
The Villa
Farleigh Wick
Nr Bath
Wiltshire BA15 2PY
Tel: 01225 851354

Wax Lyrical
(Candles, lamp oils, etc)
Tel: 020 8879 3905 for
branches
www.waxlyrical.co.uk

PAINTS

Auro Organic Paints
Pamphillions Farm
Debden
Saffron Walden
Essex CB11 3JT
Tel: 01799 543077
www.auroorganic.co.uk

Casa Paint Company
PO Box 77
Thame
Oxfordshire OX9 3FZ
Tel: 01296 770139
www.casa.co.uk

Cole & Son
142-144 Offord Road
London N1 1NS
Tel: 020 7607 4288
www.cole-and-son.com

Dulux
Tel: 01753 550555 for local
stockists
www.dulux.co.uk

Farrow & Ball
33 Uddens Trading Estate
Wimbourne
Dorset BH21 7NL
Tel: 01202 876141
www.farrow-ball.com

Fired Earth
Twyford Mill
Adderbury
Banbury
Oxfordshire OX17 3HP
Tel: 01295 814300
www.firedearth.co.uk

Jane Churchill
118 Garratt Lane
London SW18 4DJ
Tel: 020 8877 6400

**National Paint & Coatings
Association**
1500 Rhode Island NW
Washington DC 20005
USA
Tel: 202 462 6272
www.paint.org

Nutshell Natural Paints
PO Box 72
South Brent
Devon TQ10 9YR
Tel: 01364 73801
www.nutshellpaints.com

Old Fashioned Milk Paint Co
436 Main Street
PO Box 222
Groton MA 01450
USA
Tel: 978 448 6336
www.milkpaint.com

**Paint & Decorating Retailers
of America**
403 Axminister Drive
St Louis MO 63026-2941
USA
Tel: 636 326 2636
www.pdra.org

Paint and Paper Library
5 Elystan Street
London SW3 3NT
Tel: 020 7823 7755

Papers & Paints
4 Park Walk
London SW10 0AD
Tel: 020 7352 8626

RIBBONS AND TRIMMINGS

**John Lewis Department
Stores**
Tel: 020 7629 7711 for
branches
www.johnlewis.com

V V Rouleaux
54 Sloane Square
Cliveden Place
London SW1W 8AX
Tel: 020 7730 3125
www.vvrouleaux.com

STAMPS AND STENCILS

The English Stamp Company
Worth Matravers
Dorset
BH19 3JP
Tel: 01929 439117
www.englishstamp.com

Ludlow Period House Shop
141 Corve Street
Ludlow
Shropshire SY8 2PG
Tel: 01584 877276
www.periodhouseshops.com

Pavilion Originals
6a Howe Street
Edinburgh EH3 6TD
Tel: 0131 225 3590

TILES

Criterion Tiles
2a England's Lane
London NW3 4TG
Tel: 020 7483 2608
www.criterion-tiles.co.uk

**European Reclamation &
Historic Tile Co**
4524 Brazil Street
Los Angeles CA 90039
USA
Tel: 848 241 2152
www.historictile.com

Fired Earth
Twyford Mill
Oxford Road
Adderbury
Oxfordshire OX17 3HP
Tel: 01295 812088
www.firedearth.co.uk

Marlborough Tiles
Elcot Lane
Marlborough
Wiltshire SN8 2AY
Tel: 01672 512422
www.marlborough-tiles.co.uk

The Oxford Tile Shop
22 Park End Street
Oxford OX1 1HU
Tel: 01865 200205

Reject Tile Shop
196 Wandsworth Bridge Road
London SW6 2UF
Tel: 020 7736 9610
www.criterion-tiles.co.uk

Tile Council of America
100 Clemson Research
Blvd Anderson
SC29625
USA
Tel: 864 646 8453 or
805 237 2375
www.tileusa.com

World's End Tiles
Silverthorne Road
London SW8 3HE
Tel: 020 7819 2110
www.worldsendtiles.co.uk

Wallpapers

Brunschwig & Fils
10 The Chambers
Chelsea Harbour Drive
London SW10 0XF
Tel: 020 7351 5797
www.brunschwig.com

Clarence House Fabrics
3/10 Chelsea Harbour Design
Centre
London SW10 OXE
Tel: 020 7351 1200
www.clarencehouse.com

Colefax and Fowler
19-23 Grosvenor Hill
London W1X 9HG
Tel: 020 7493 2231

Jane Churchill
81 Pimlico Road
London SW1W 8PH
Tel: 020 7730 8654

Sanderson
100 Acres
Sanderson Road
Uxbridge
Middlesex UB8 1DH
Tel: 01895 201509

Zoffany
Talbot House
17 Church Road
Rickmansworth
Hertfordshire WD3 1DF
Tel: 01923 710680

Wooden Furniture, Plain and
Painted

Angela Page
11 Little Mount Sion
Tunbridge Wells
Kent TN1 1YS
Tel: 01892 522217

**The Arts and Crafts
Furniture Company**
49 Sheen Lane
London SW14 8AB
Tel: 020 8876 6544
www.acfc.co.uk

The Blue Door
74 Church Road
London SW13 0DQ
Tel: 020 8748 9785

The Dining Room Shop
62-4 White Hart Lane
London SW13 0PZ
Tel: 020 8878 1020

The Granary
31 High Street
Watlington
Oxfordshire OX49 5PZ
Tel: 01491 612530

Grand Illusions
41 Crown Road
St Margaret's
Twickenham
Middlesex TW1 3EJ
Tel: 020 8607 9446

Laura Ashley
Tel: 0990 622116 for branches
www.lauraashley.com

Maine Cottage
PO Box 935
Yarmouth ME 04096
USA
Tel: 207 846 1430
www.mainecottage.com

New Heights
289 Cricklewood Broadway
London NW2 6NX
Tel: 020 8452 1500

**The Real Wood Furniture
Company**
16 Oxford Street
Woodstock
Oxfordshire OX20 1TS
Tel: 01993 813887

Sabrina
(Oak doors)
Alma Street
Mountfields
Shrewsbury
Shropshire SY3 8QL
Tel: 01743 357977

Scumble Goosie
(Ready-to-paint furniture and
accessories)
Lewiston Mill
Toadsmoor Road
Stroud
Gloucestershire GL5 2TB
Tel: 01453 731305
www.scumble-goosie.co.uk

The Shaker Shop
72-3 Marylebone High Street
London W1U 5JW
Tel: 020 7935 9461
www.shaker.co.uk

All information current at the
time of publication. Neither the
publisher nor companies listed
can be held responsible for
errors or subsequent changes.